CW00684169

Published
by Kirkbymoorside History Group
2010

With thanks to all the former employees and patients who
helped with this booklet and to all those who supported this
project.

Cover photograph by W Hayes courtesy of the
Ryedale Folk Museum, Hutton-le-Hole.

Adela Bartlaw

Before embarking on the history of the hospital it may be helpful to know a little of the background of one key figure - Adela Shaw.

She was born Adela Constance Alexandrina Durrant in Marylebone, Middlesex in 1869, the daughter of Sir Henry Josias Durrant, 4th Baronet. and Alexandrina Charlotte Barton.

James Edward Shaw was the second son of John Shaw, farmer and governing director of the South Kirby Colliery Company. The couple married on 27 July 1892 and initially lived at Barnby Dunn near Doncaster. However with the purchase of Welburn Estate in 1894 James and Adela Shaw relocated to Welburn Manor.

The Shaw family had, and still have, a long connection with the military. James E Shaw served in the Kings Own Yorkshire Light Infantry and saw action in the Boer War. Sadly he died in October 1911, leaving behind Adela to care for four children. The family-owned collieries in South Kirby, Featherstone and Hemsworth raised platoons to serve in WWI and the wholesale devastation of a generation had an overwhelming impact on the Shaw family as it did with countless others.

Welburn Hall, their family home, had been used for the treatment and recuperation of wounded soldiers and the family's commitment to supporting the care of those wounded in the Great War would continue beyond the end of the conflict itself. As well as her commitment to the hospitals in Kirbymoorside Adela was also President of the Yorkshire Association of Women's Institutes, a huge movement at this time. She also held the office of Justice of the Peace (JP) for the North Riding, Yorkshire in 1921 and in 1930 she was invested as a Commander, Order of the British Empire (C.B.E). In later life she moved to Burn Hall near York and lived to the age of 92. Adela Shaw died on 16 December 1962.

This begins as her story.

Hayes

The first hospital to appear in Kirbymoorside that Mrs Adela Shaw was involved with was the RYEDALE COTTAGE HOSPITAL. It was built on the small site at the north side of Howkeld and was designed and built by Ernest Burrowes just after the First World War. Mrs Shaw sponsored the construction of the building alongside Lady Margaret Beckett and Mrs Harrison Holt.

The hospital was officially opened by Lady Bell in 1920; she gave a eulogy and opened the building with a gold-chasted key watched by a large crowd. The hospital itself comprised of two wards and three individual bedrooms in the care of a matron, Miss Charlotte Julia Horton, and a servant. Its purpose was to care for patients who had undergone surgical operations in town but who could not be nursed at home; it was not meant to accommodate infectious or chronic cases. The Cottage Hospital was entirely supported by donations and subscriptions from the townspeople so fund-raising events were needed to defray costs. Such events included a gramophone evening with selection of music and a dance, some events being more successful than others. When the traveling fair came to Kirbymoorside at Michelmas (Nov 1922) one of the women broke her leg and was treated at the Cottage Hospital. In recognition of the care she received at the time, the fair donated a night's takings towards the building's upkeep for many years after.

The hospital served the locality well for sixteen years but in 1936 a meeting was called to consider its closure. Mr. W H F Hoodless, who had been secretary for sixteen years, reported that the operating cost for 1935/36 had been £420; the Shaw family offsetting £320 towards this. Essential building repairs would cost £600 and would have meant an increase in subscriptions to 6/- a year. Scarborough Hospital, which had been recently opened, served as a good alternative with an ambulance service for the local people. Dr. Walsh Tetley was opposed to the closure, arguing that the hospital provided beds in the event of a shortage elsewhere. However the closure of the hospital was proposed and subsequently effected. During the Second World War Matron Charlotte Julia Horton became a sister at the Welburn Hall Convalescent Hospital.

Left: Crowds gathered at Howkeld to see the opening of the Ryedale Cottage Hospital August 26 1920

Hayes

The hospital building can still be seen on the A170 today, opposite Howkeld on the road to Helmsley. From the outside it looks unchanged and has now been converted into houses.

Sir – With reference to the appeal for funds to establish in Yorkshire a hospital school for Crippled Children - it is with much pleasure I am able to announce that Mrs Edward Shaw of Welburn Manor has offered her hospital at Kirbymoorside previously used as a Red Cross hospital for ex-servicemen, for at least 5 years at a nominal rent of 1s 1d per year. This will provide an excellent beginning, capable of expansion as experience may suggest and will form the nucleus of the Yorkshire County Orthopaedic Hospital.

This property consists of 4 large army huts together with an adjacent stone bungalow. The ward accommodation for children would be about 70 - 100 beds. All the buildings are most compact and complete, with water born sanitation, beds, electric light, kitchen, etc. The land available allows for considerable expansion.

Mrs Shaw's most generous offer – which is free from all restrictions – has been accepted by the executive committee.

The urgency is great. There are in Yorkshire about 5000 children of school age, now crippled, the vast majority of whom are wholly or partially curable, with proper treatment. Sir Robert Jones, the well known orthopaedic surgeon, has stated that 80% of cripples if treated early enough can be cured. There are at present only 250 beds in Yorkshire hospitals and institutions allocated for such cases and in these, except for two instances, there is no provision for education. A hospital school where cure and education are simultaneously obtainable is a crying need. Such is provided in other counties with highly successful results, and surely Yorkshire cannot be indifferent to an appeal for those so suffering and so helpless.

On behalf of the Yorkshire Federation for Maternity and Child Welfare I make an earnest appeal for money, goods in kind – such as coal, flour, groceries, etc., parcels of linen, cots and bedding, and toys, etc.

Let it never be said that Yorkshire failed in anything she put her hand to; she is good at cricket and "playing the game", and she should be good at attacking the cure of cripples.

Subscriptions should be sent to The Manager, Barclays Bank, York or to me at this office, and gifts in kind to Mrs Edward Shaw, OBE, JP, the Red Cross Hospital, Kirbymoorside. – Yours Truly,

R.L Bower, Major,
Chairman, Executive Committee.
The Red Cross Office, Northallerton,
1st July 1924.

The above appeal was published in the York Herald in 1924. We understand t h a t some of the terms and phrases used in this booklet may cause offence in today's world. However they are taken verbatim from written and published sources and should be read in historical context.

Major **Sir Robert Lister Bower** was born in 1860 and was a British Army, colonial and police officer who served as Chief Constable of the North Riding of Yorkshire Constabulary from 1898 until his death in 1929.

He came from an old Yorkshire family; his father was Robert Hartley Bower of Welham Hall, Malton and his mother was a daughter of Sir John Lister-Kaye, 2nd Baronet of Denby Grange. Commissioned into the Kerry Militia, he then transferred to the King's Royal Rifle Corps in 1881. Serving in the Egyptian campaign of 1882, the 1884 Sudan campaign and the Nile Expeditions of 1884 -1885, he was mentioned in dispatches three times. He also served with the Jebu expedition in West Africa and was Political Officer at Jebu Ode. For these services he was appointed Companion of the Order of St Michael and St George (CMG) in 1897. Back in England he was appointed Chief Constable of the North Riding of Yorkshire in 1898. During World War One he returned to the Army as Deputy Assistant Adjutant-General in Egypt and was later appointed Commander of the Order of the British Empire (CBE) in the 1920 civilian war honours. Sir Bower was promoted to Knight Commander (KBE) in the 1925 Birthday Honours.

Obituary 15 June 1929

This was the background of the man who began his campaign to establish the Yorkshire Children's Orthopaedic Hospital.

5

Yorkshire Children's Orthopaedic Hospital

1924 saw the start of the project which was to become a life-long commitment for Adela Shaw and would make her name synonymous with child welfare in Yorkshire. Proposed at a time of upheaval following the end of the Great War (1914 -1918), the Shaw family had already been involved with the Red Cross movement. In 1919 the family built a Pensioners' hospital on land owned on Westfields. It operated as an auxiliary hospital to the one at Leeds, the Beckett Park Hospital. Many of those who needed care had, by 1924, moved either back home or to more permanent care facilities and The Ministry of Pensions decreed the site was no longer needed.

KIRBYMOORSIDE RED + CONVALESCENT HOMES   Hayes

However, by this time another urgent need had been identified by the medical profession – that of the treatment for thousands of children who suffered from surgical TB, rickets and Polio (infantile paralysis). This area of medicine had been neglected in Yorkshire through lack of specialist knowledge, facilities and care. Surgeons had until now only dealt with the disease and could not address the after effects and disabilities which even then could be prevented if the children were seen early enough. The aim of the new hospital site at Kirbymoorside was to address all aspects of the child's health and development. Not only would they treat the disease but also educate the children, support their recovery and follow up on their after-care through a network of clinics. This approach of total care had already been introduced in eight other counties and the need in Yorkshire was no less urgent with around 5000 known cases, 1/20th of all children in Yorkshire, only 250 beds available. With areas such as Teesside with heavy steel industries and West

Yorkshire with its milling factories, Sir Robert Bower, in his radio appeal for donations, [*BBC Leeds & Bradford Broadcast 2/3/26*] blasted the failure of society to take responsibility:

"...one of the many features of our modern elaborate civilisation is our aptitude for manufacture, and during the last century the pursuit of knowledge, of the working side by side with industry, has resulted in achievements of which man has just reason to be proud. But there has also arisen such a wholesale manufacture of cripples that if generous measures for the care, and prevention of crippledom, are not promptly taken it will rebound to our everlasting shame. For it is the rule that cripples are made not born. It is true that a small proportion of them are born defective, but adequate treatment in early infancy makes the rectification of these defects simple. The bulk of our cripples are produced in the factory of our civilisation by the machinery of dirt, neglect, overcrowding, bad feeding, lack of sunshine and lack of fresh air. We have all seen in our large cities children hobbling about with hideously distorted limbs, the result of rickets. Rickets is caused by improper and insufficient feeding, combined with lack of sunshine and fresh air. Its cure is simple but during the active stage of the disease the bones become soft and spongy, and bend, or even break under the bodyweight. TB very commonly affects the bones and joints of young children and the undoubted curative effects of sunshine and fresh air make it unnecessary to seek further for its most potent cause. In some of our cripples the cause is purely incidental. The so-called infantile paralysis is an epidemic in the same way that scarlet fever and measles are epidemics, but whereas most children recover from these with no untoward permanent results, infantile paralysis is apt to leave muscles, groups of muscles, or even whole limbs, withered and useless."

It would be easy to blame social conditions alone, but the local population in Ryedale was no less exposed to such diseases. What Ryedale did have to offer according to Dr G R Girdlestone, an Oxford surgeon and clinical consultant, was **".....a healthy and bracing part of North Riding, noted for its pure and dry air"** which at the time he believed to be essential as he also commented that **"...the sky, the wind and the gleams of the sun were better than artificial sun"**. Although others disagreed with the location, the offer of the site by Mrs Adela Shaw, following the initial plea from the Federation of Maternity and Child Welfare in Yorkshire, was such that this project could be made reality. The site had the basics of water and electricity and the wooden buildings were already in place, complete with land for expansion and a stone cottage for the staff. Initially Mrs Shaw gave the site on a five-year lease at a nominal rent of 1s 1d per year.

Aerial View of the hospital site

With the site decided upon, the drive for funding became urgent as it was estimated that the project would cost around £14,000 to make it reality.

Appeals for donations were made through the press, the radio and by sending letters out to local authorities, hospitals, as well as the landed gentry and families of wealth. Some of the donations came from the less obvious sources. The Ainderby Girl Guides donated £6 7s 2d as a result of their carol singing, entertainments and sale of work; the colliers from the pits at Hemsworth, Featherstone, South Kirby [Pontefract] raised £500; and Captain and Mrs Taylor held a garden party at Sutton Hall in Thirsk where the highlight was the 8th Kings Royal Irish Hussars. Closer to home the Hunt Meet at Welburn Manor raised 15 guineas at a whist drive, a dance at Oswaldkirk raised £21 5s 6d and Mr Turton local MP donated £5, as did Admiral and Mrs Fuller of Douthwaite Dale. When it was noted that there was little interest coming in from the West Riding Sir Neville Wilkinson, whose beautiful Titania's Palace was being exhibited in Sheffield, donated £144 8s - half the admissions which were shared between the Yorkshire Children's Orthopaedic Hospital and King Edward VII Orthopaedic Hospital, Rivelin Valley, Sheffield. Titania's Palace was a magnificent miniature Palace commissioned by Sir Neville Wilkinson at the request of his young daughter as home fit for the fairies in which all young girls believe. It took 15 years to make and housed 3,000 miniature works of art. Today it lives in the Eskerov Castle Museum in Denmark.

Titania's Palace on display today.
Pictures courtesy of the Egeskov Museum, Denmark

The totals grew steadily -

September 1924	£1,801	December	£2,807
October	£2,141	January 1925	£3,019
November	£2,448		

At a concert and tea given at Ribston Hall, 170 guests were entertained and then reminded that 100 bankers' orders were at the door waiting to be filled in. The funds then received a huge boost with a donation of £5000 from Right Hon TR Ferens of Hull. Thomas Robinson Ferens was a wealthy businessman and Liberal MP for Hull, but his roots were very different. Born in 1847, son of a Durham miller, Thomas Ferens had arrived in Hull with two shillings and then worked his way to success, up through the ranks of the Reckitt & Sons Co., where he finally became chairman. His Methodist upbringing meant that for him, wealth should be used to benefit others and his donation to the hospital was one of many he made throughout his life, including £500,000 to build and develop the site of Hull University.

Thomas R Ferens

However the money came with a proviso; that the hospital must take cases from the East Riding, where there was a great need for such treatment. The board readily agreed and the first ideas of the layout for the hospital began to take shape. Work began shortly after Christmas 1924 and there was a great deal of work to be done to bring the wooden buildings up to the required standard for the care and education of sick children and the staff requirements of such a hospital.

Architect's Report – February 1925 *Yorkshire Post*:

Isolation Block – on the northern boundary, entirely apart from the main block and contains four wards, duty rooms, and the necessary conveniences.

Wards – it is suggested the three wards be named the North Riding, East Riding, and West Riding. Each ward will contain 35 beds, planned with a southern aspect, with veranda and lawn in front.

Operative Block – the Operative Block is placed on the east side of the three wards, and contains day room, teachers' rooms, gymnasium, stores, plaster room, anaesthetic room, nurses' room, x-ray room, dark room, post-operative room (one for each sex). The whole of the above rooms will be fitted replete with all the present up-to-date appliances requisite to do the work required and has been planned and arranged after careful examination of several hospitals in the country.

Staff Quarters – is detached from the main block, connected with same by covered ways, and contains bedrooms, kitchen, etc necessary to house the working staff of the hospital.

The resident surgeon will reside in a newly erected stone bungalow, which contains sitting room, three bedrooms, kitchen, bathroom, etc, and is situated at the south-east corner of the staff quarters.

The whole of the buildings will be heated on the low pressure gravity system, using hospital type radiators and of sufficient capacity to keep a uniform temperature.

The plans have been approved by the Board of Education [Medical Branch] and it is hoped that the hospital will be ready for re-opening in May 1925.

The site is situated some 200 feet above the sea level in a healthy bracing part of the North Riding, which is noted for its pure and dry air all the year round; and when complete will contain all the latest Sanitary Lighting, and Heating arrangements.

GARSIDE & PENNINGTON
Architects and Surveyors
Pontefract Yorkshire
December 1924

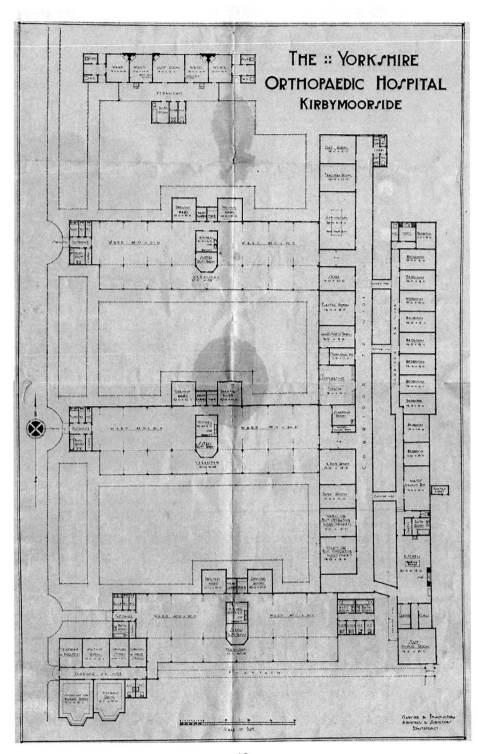

THE :: YORKSHIRE
ORTHOPAEDIC HOSPITAL
KIRBYMOORSIDE

SCALE OF FEET

The committee, set up to run the hospital project and co-ordinate its development, consisted of the following:

Major Robert L Bower, CMG, CBE {Chairman Hospital Committee & County Director North Riding Branch, Order of St John & CRBS}
Lady Bell, DBE; JP {President North Riding Branch, British Red Cross Society}
Lady Beresford-Peirse, OBE {Vice-President, North Riding Branch, Red Cross Society}
Mrs Currer-Briggs, MBE {President, Leeds Poor Children's Holiday Camp}
The Hon Sir Gervase Beckett, Bart, MP
Lady Firth, Scriven Park, Knaresborough
Dr S Fox-Linten, MSC; DPH {Medical Officer of Health, Scarborough}
Dr JR Kaye, CM; DPH {County Medical Officer, West Riding}
Robina, Viscountess Mount Garret, OBE {Vice President, West Riding Branch, Order of St. John}
Brig.-General H. Mendes, CB {County Director, West Riding Branch, Order of St John}
Dr H Mason, DPH {County Medical Officer, North Riding}
Mrs Leslie Richmond, Ripley Harrogate.
Mrs Edward Shaw, OBE, JP {Vice-President North Riding Branch, British Red Cross Society}
Lady Sykes, Sledmere, Malton
Dr RL Thornley, DPH {County Medical Officer, East Riding}
Dr AEL Wear, CMG {Schools Medical Officer, Leeds}

The knowledge, influence and respected position in society of the above people were essential to bring the hospital to fruition; without such backing the hospital, however worthy a cause, could not have drawn in enough support both financial and political. Even with their connections the board members had to fight the hospital's corner through the media and the government, to ensure that those who were able to help did so.

With a deadline in sight the hospital had to be furnished and staff had to be appointed. The closure of the Biddulph Grange Charity Hospital, due to lack of funding, meant that the equipment there was sold en bloc, a windfall for the Kirbymoorside site. The operating theatre, plaster room and beds and cots all had to be bought and with £12,000 raised, the push for opening began. The outside work was put out to tender and many local tradesmen bid for contracts. The following were successful -

Brickwork and Road-laying	£3,600	Ernest Burrowes
Joinery	£4,900	Harry Rivis
Heating and Lighting	£ 950	Messrs Russell & Co
Plumbing and Glazing	£3,834	J Whittaker, Easingwold

In addition the following won tenders for the first six month orders of supplies:

Coal	J Walton & Co, Middlesbrough
Beef, mutton & pork	Mr G Wilson, Nawton
Groceries	Mr Hill & Co/ Mr Sunley, KMS
Milk	Mr G Warriner, Welburn
	Mr J Cussons, Hagg Farm, KMS

For a hospital it was obvious that there was need for an ambulance but as Sir Robert Bower discovered, on making enquiries in York in 1925, there was only one in use and that was owned by the police. Again Mrs Shaw came to the rescue by offering use of her Red Cross ambulance for children who were unable to reach the town by train. Those arriving by train would need a taxi to come from the station.

Rules for the admission of children had to be decided upon and a fee for their treatment and education agreed with the Ministries of Health and Education. The following regulations were issued by Sir R Bower in 1925:

1. Applicants must be suffering from some defect tending to produce crippling, but only those cases will be admitted in which there is a reasonable prospect of cure or alleviation. Chronic or incurable cases cannot be admitted.

2. Until otherwise determined by the Committee, no child under the age of 3 nor over the age of 12 years will be eligible for admission.

3. Suitable patients will be admitted in the order of their

application.

4. The Honorary Surgical Officers and the Resident Surgical Officer shall be sole judges as to whether a patient is both suitable for admission and treatment.

5. Parents or Guardians or Authorities responsible for the treatment of cases shall enter into an agreement to pay an inclusive charge of 52/6 per week.

6. Applications in writing for admission must be made to the Resident Surgical Officer who will supply a form to be filled up by the applicant's Medical Attendant.

7. Parents and Guardians will be required to provide a certificate, or other evidence of the child's freedom from contagious or infectious illness, and that such child has not been in contact during the four weeks previous to admission with or resident in a house where there is, or has been during the same period, infectious disease.

8. The following is a list of articles to be sent with the patients

3 night gowns	Comb
3 pairs bed socks	Tooth brush
3 night shirts or pyjamas	Tooth powder
3 warm vests	

NB Garments made of flannelette not permissible.

9. Patients must conform rigidly to the rules of the hospital.

10. Visiting days will be once every month. Two adults only will be allowed to visit on the days mentioned. Food, fruit, etc, must be handed to the Matron.

11. An undertaking shall in every case be given by parents that on discharge and when deemed necessary, patients shall attend at a stated time an After-Care Clinic for the purpose of re-examination, and if necessary further

treatment at the After-Care Clinic.

12. Apparatus loaned to patients on discharge shall be returned to the Hospital when no longer necessary for the treatment and parents or guardians shall be responsible for any damage or loss thereto.

13. Parents or Authorities responsible for the treatment shall provide in part or whole the cost of any special apparatus deemed necessary, at the direction of the Committee.

September 1925

The question of staffing had to be decided and the first appointments made in July 1925 were as follows:

Senior Hon Consulting Orthopaedic Surgeon –

        Sir Robert Jones, KBE, CB Liverpool

Honorary Orthopaedic Surgeon:	Mr S Daw, Leeds
Surgeons:	Mr J Hall (Bradford),
	Mr J G Craig (York),
	Mr H D Levick (Middlesbrough)
Honorary Consultant Physicians:	Dr C Vining
Honorary Medical Officers:	Dr T Walsh-Tetley (Kirbymoorside)
	Dr R Jackson (Kirbymoorside)
Honorary Ophthalmic Surgeon:	Mr Lodge (Halifax)
Honorary Dentist:	Mr Calder (Helmsley)

However the key figure in the hospital was to be a man appointed as the resident surgical officer; a man described by Sir Robert Bower as **"a young and rising orthopaedic surgeon who is likely to make a big name for himself"** - Howard Crockatt. He himself had suffered from poliomyelitis as a child and had a great empathy with these children. As a resident of Leeds he grew up very aware of the problems facing families and children who were suffering and had graduated from Leeds Medical School in 1919. He worked in Leeds General Infirmary before taking up the post of surgeon in Kirbymoorside. In his view orthopaedic surgery had more to offer these children than most other branches of surgery.

The matron appointed to take charge of the nursing staff, all of whom were single women, was Miss L Poole who had previously been matron at the Ethel Hedley Hospital, Windermere at a salary of £150 per annum including board, laundry and uniform allowance (£10 pa). An advert was placed for **"a good plain cook"** at a salary of £50 per annum and Mrs Shaw had found a suitable man who could attend the boilers, electrics, lights and the garden at a salary of 50/- per week – Mr K Walker of Kirbymoorside. He was to be assisted by Mr Russell in the gardens and was in 1928 joined by Mr Thomas Scaling of Kirbymoorside, who was an engineer and started on 1 February at a salary of £5 10/- a year to work primarily with the boilers.

The grand opening of the hospital took place on Friday 31 July 1925 when HRH Princess Mary Viscountess Lascelles agreed to perform the inaugural ceremony. Along with the new drive, the hospital had to construct a platform on the west front of the west wing to allow everyone a view of the royal visitor and a marquee was erected to serve teas to the 600 guests. The event was described in full detail by a woman journalist from the *Yorkshire Herald*:-

Sir Robert Bower (left) escorting Princess Mary with Sir Hugh Bell (right)

"[Princess Mary]...was met at the gaily decorated hospital gates by Major Sir Robert Bower; Sir Hugh Bell, Lord Lieutenant of the North Riding, and Lady Bell; Mrs Edward Shaw and a number of the members of the hospital committee - among them Dr Algernon Wear, the Chairman of the Leeds Committee – all of whom were presented to her. On her way up the drive, she inspected a guard of honour formed by girl guides and another by members of the VAD;

and stopped for a moment to speak to Mrs John Shaw, who, in her attractive crimson uniform, was in command.

A slender figure in a straight frock of pavlova mauve, georgette belt and floating panels embroidered in needle-run knots, the Princess then passed to the platform, followed by her lady-in-waiting, Miss Cybil Kenyon-Slaney, in a pretty embroidered frock and a navy hat. Here, Miss Margaret Shaw followed and presented to Princess Mary a simple posy bouquet of mauve sweet peas and fern fronds, tied with narrow ribbons. The opening ceremony lasted but a short time. Sir Robert Bower made a brief opening speech, and he was followed by Dr Wear, who explained in admirably concise fashion how the hospital had originated. Princess Mary then unlocked the door with a golden key, and the building was dedicated by the Archbishop of York.

1. Sir Henry Beresford Peirse 2. Mrs E Shaw 3. Archbishop of York 4. Sir Robert Bower 5. Lady Bell 6. Mrs Jack Shaw 7. Countess of Lindsay 8. Rt Hon TR Ferens 9. Lady Dorothy Wood & Capt J Shaw 10. Margaret Shaw 11. Earl of Feversham & Earl of Lindsay 12. Lady Marjorie Beckett 13. Lady Syke 14. Sir Hugh Bell

Group Photo Outside Welburn Manor 31 July 1925.

After the Princess had walked through the wards, she returned to the platform where she was thanked, first by Sir Hugh Bell, and then by the Archbishop, who assured her that Yorkshire had taken her into its ample and warm heart and that he hoped that she would remain there for many years....Lady Marjorie Becket, in a patterned georgette frock of white and violet, was among Princess Mary's supporters on the platform; as were Lady Dorothy Wood, in a navy silk frock and coat; Lady Sykes in black with a small mauve hat; and Lady Bell, in black. Mrs Shaw wore a smart two-piece costume with pretty motifs of coloured embroidery, and Mrs Currer-Briggs was in pale grey."

Princess Mary's interest in the hospital was real as she was already the President of The Yorkshire Federation for Maternity and Child Welfare and knew much about the techniques and treatment of infantile diseases.

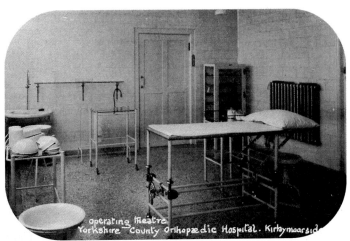

operating theatre
Yorkshire County Orthopædic Hospital. Kirbymoorside

Hayes

The first child patients arrived on 1 October 1925 and by the end of the first financial year the hospital offered 103 beds and had treated 59 patients, five of whom had already gone home. At this point Mrs Shaw extended the lease on the site to a 99 year lease at a charge of 1/1d per year which now included use of the two cottages and part of the large field beside the hospital. The hospital board continued to appeal for funds as the need for bigger, better and newer equipment came to light. The people of Kirbymoorside under the lead of Dr Walsh-Tetley raised £50 to purchase a Hawley Plaster table and the annual reports published by the hospital show just how much they relied on public generosity, with annual subscriptions forming the backbone of this support. The following, listed in the 1929 Annual End of Year Report for the Hospital, showed donations for the children at Christmas in 1928 :

Xmas Gifts

Beckett, Lady Marjorie	Goose
Bower, Lady	£3 3s 6d for toys
Bower, Sir Robert	Crackers and Chocolate
Booth, Misses	Motor car and large doll's pram
Burrowes, Mr	£1
Bucktin, Miss FE	Meccano sets
Carter, Miss	Games
Courage, Mrs	6 shirts
Charter, Miss	Toys
Clarke, Mrs	Cakes
Cussons, Mr	Turkey
Cudworth, Miss	Books
Easingwold VADs	Toys and Clothes
Ellis, Mrs	Games
Fife, Mrs	Games and Books
Frank, Miss C	Dolls and punch
Frank, Miss C	Dolls
Fuller, Admiral Sir C	Toys
Gethin, Colonel and Mrs	Toys and Games
Gothorp, Mrs	Toys and Sweets
Gjers, Mrs	Toys, dolls, etc.
Hartley, Mrs	10/-
Harome Bethlehem Tableaux	Toys and Games
Hildyard, Master	Toys
Holden, the Lady	2 bottles of sweets
Holt, Mrs Harrison	Toys, oranges and 'Xmas tree
Husthwaite, WI	Cushions
Huskinson, Mrs	Games, scrap books
Jackson, Miss	Toys and dolls
Kirbymoorside WI	Teddy bear
Lancaster, Mrs	Box of oranges
Legard, Mrs	Toys
Mason, Dr	200 crackers
Mountgarrett, Lady	Case of oranges
Northallerton VADs	Toys
Parish, S	£1

Pearson, Mrs	Rabbits
Pickering C of E. School	Toys
Powell, Miss	Toys and crackers
Punshon, Mrs	Truck of Coal
Rivis, Mr	Barrel of apples
Richardson, Mrs	Tin of sweets
Royen, Mr	'Xmas tree
Sample, Mrs	Tin of sweets
Shaw, Mrs JED	13 doz. boxes of chocolates
Shaw, Mrs Edward	£5 for toys
Sheppey, Mrs	Toys
Sowerby – 1st Rangers	Toys
Swinton VADs	Toys and Chocolates
Tunstall, Mrs	£1 1s 0d
Turton, Lady	Toys
Walker, Mrs C	10/-
Warren, Sir Digby	Cases of oranges & apples
Wyvill, Mrs D'Arcy	Games, clothes and toys

As well as the gifts which came in for the special events, the hospital published lists of donations each year in the Annual Reports until 1942, listing everything which came in, even the mundane eg

Mrs Allenby	- Hot cross buns and bread
British Legion	- Balloons
Sir G Beckett	- Grouse (given each year)
Mrs Harden	- Sunhats
Mrs Mends	- Woollies and bedsocks
Mr H Rivis	- Cask of grapes
Mrs C Walker	- Gooseberries and marrows

Other regular donations came in from the surrounding parish churches at Harvest Festival time when they sent in the fruit, vegetables, flowers, jams and eggs, all of which were gratefully received by the children, who often came in need of wholesome and fresh foods as well as medical care. Legacies were also sent to the Board to keep the hospital running; one such local resident, Mr Joseph Duck of Farndale, remembered the children in his will in 1942 and the minutes note he left £45 for their care. One other remarkable gift was listed in 1930 – Mr Coupland of Collingham gave a Daimler car for use as an ambulance. The hospital had to use the Red Cross vehicle donated by Mrs Shaw until they were able purchase an Austin Ambulance in 1936 at a cost of £500. However it is interesting to note that the Chief Constable for the North Riding Police wrote to the hospital in 1932, reminding them that they were not permitted to display the Red Cross on the vehicles and it should be removed forthwith.

Some of the child patients lined up on the boys' ward.

These beds could be pushed outside so the patients could get even more fresh air and sunshine if weather allowed

Adela's involvement in the running of the committee grew when she was nominated as Chairman of the Board, following the sudden death of Sir Robert Bowers from pneumonia at his home in Thirsk in June 1929.

With rising patient and staffing levels, space was at a premium. An extra block of 18 bedrooms and two sitting rooms was added to the nursing accommodation. In 1929 a recreation hut was added along with lawns and a tennis court. In 1926 Dr Crockatt married and two years later moved into a new house in the grounds called "Rahane." - a name in memory of childhood holidays spent at Meikle Rahane near Helensburgh above Glasgow in Scotland. A laundry block was built in 1928 to reduce costs by keeping the domestic services as in-house as possible; the same reasoning resulted in the creation of the splint shop in 1931. The inevitable first death in the hospital also prompted the building of a mortuary block, well out of sight of the little patients in the wards. The old buildings needed re-decorating and re-roofing. Local tradesmen tendered for the contract of painting the corridors -

Mr Marmaduke Place   £130
Mr Bert Boddy   £137

The cheapest tender won.

However the costs for re-roofing were prohibitive and so the Board decided to have the roofs painted with red rubberine in 1933 at a cost of £53 10/- to try to prolong the life of the buildings.

With the relaxation of the age for young admissions, the need for a dedicated block to house the babies was identified to treat those up to the age of four. Again Dr Crockatt believed that many of the malformed bones would respond well if treated at a very early stage, a view seen as the norm in today's world. Funds had to be raised again and a fête was organised in the hospital grounds, bringing in £400.

Opened on 1 August 1935 by Viscountess Halifax, in glorious sunshine the guests were treated to teas in a marquee, and the following list of local stallholders appeared in the *Yorkshire Herald* –

Antique stall	Lady Marjorie Beckett
Produce stall	Mrs Shaw, Mrs Gordon Foster, Mrs RD Fife
Toiletries stall	Miss Buckton
Sweets stall	Miss Baring, Miss Holt
Cake stall	Mrs Waind, Mrs Rivis
Mystery stall	Mrs T Waind, Miss V Rivis
Kitchen stall	Mrs Crockatt, Mrs Hanks, Mrs Stewart Mrs Tweedie

Refreshments	Mrs Galloway, Miss Tweedie
Side-shows	Miss C Frank, Mr F Linton, Capt C Scott-Hopkins,
	Miss Bromley, Mrs Kennedy, Mr RT Smith

Appeals for the new building were made raising another £300 and the Northern Regional Children's Radio Circle donated £500 towards the costs. There there was also a Baby Show which proved to be very popular. This photo by W Hayes shows some of the winners.

Built of brick and made to last, the new Babies Ward or Ward IV, was officially opened by Olive Shapley, the well known radio presenter and producer for Children's Hour, on 29th December 1936. At the same time the new isolation block was built, bringing the cost of works to a total of £3,330. This burden meant that at the outbreak of the war the hospital had a budget deficit.

The teaching staff on site had a high turnover rate; the first headmistress Miss PM Nield, recruited on 1 December 1925 resigned in March 1926. She was followed by Miss Marion Dyson of Wetherby, in July 1926. She worked hard with the first child patients and all of those over the age of seven years received formal lessons. In 1927 she applied to the Board for funding for a course of basketry and was granted the permission to keep any profits from the sale of the boys' work. The boys under 10 made stools, bookcases and cane-edged trays whilst the girls did sewing, embroidery and rugs. By 1928 they had raised £12 10/-, enough to buy a piano for their entertainment. However her job became increasingly challenging and in 1927 a plea came for assistance to help cope with **the discipline in the school as the bigger boys were apt to get out of hand out of school hours and are inclined to be troublesome.** The Board acknowledged this by recruiting two other teachers – Miss Barnes and Miss Laidlaw – as well as purchasing a wooden shed for the boys to use as a workshop and to give their energy an outlet. Dr Crockatt also suggested that the hospital should establish a troop of Boy Scouts and Girl Guides which again met with the approval of the Board. When Miss Britton took over as headmistress, in October 1928 she continued to carry on this demanding work and in 1930 she was allowed to submit the children's efforts to an Exhibition of Works in Exeter where eight other orthopaedic hospitals

were also exhibiting. In 1932 Ms Britton resigned and Ms Rippon took over with Ms Adams, Miss Solomon, Pattinson and Miss Gardner assisting her.

Left : Boy Scouts troop 1950s

Dr Crockatt was the one constant member of staff, ably assisted by Matron Poole. By 1935 she was in charge of a site employing five sisters, 18 probationers (nurses under 18) and 12 domestic staff. Together they saw innumerable nurses and surgeons come and then move on professionally, some of whom would return. The nurses joined at age 16 as this allowed them time to gain experience in nursing before going on to take their formal nurse training at age 18. All were recruited from different parts of the country. They lived on site and were the responsibility of Matron and the sisters who ran the hospital, staff and patients, with strict efficiency and order. The hours were long and the work demanding, but no worse than those faced by many other young girls in the domestic or farming situations available to them at the time. The house surgeons were expected to work from 9 – 5 on weekdays and 9 – 1 on Saturdays and all other times to be within reasonable call. In 1936 Dr Kathleen Adamson became

Dr Howard Crockatt

house surgeon; she left but would return on 12 October 1941 and then remain as Dr Crockatt's constant support for almost another 30 years.

Dr Crockatt and his team treated a wide range of issues and a table in the 1927 Annual Report showed that in the first year they had 171 cases diagnosed with the following:

Tuberculosis of the spine, hip, knee and ankle;

Rickets	Acute Anterior Poliomyelitis
Infantile Hemiplegia	Spastic Paraplegia
Club foot	Congenital dislocation of the hip
Torticollis	Scoliosis
Knee Injuries	

In the remarks Dr Crockatt reported that operative correction of deformity was not attempted before seven yrs of age and of all the 52 non-TB cases listed eight were cured, 42 had improved and only one had not improved. The average duration of treatment for those affected by TB of the knee was 319 days. There was also a breakdown of where these cases had been referred from:

North Riding	57	East Riding	27
West Riding	61	York	12
Private/others	14		

By 1933 the hospital staff were able to compare the fluctuating caseloads and the amount of time spent at Kirbymoorside -

1931-32	TB	**60** cases averaging **541** days' stay
	Non-TB	**139** cases averaging **89** days' stay
1932-33	TB	**31** cases averaging **462** days' stay
	Non-TB	**153** cases averaging **107** days' stay

As the hospital grew so did the expertise of the staff and the equipment and techniques in use. The daily sessions using sunlight lamps were a common treatment, often for three to four hours in order to improve the tone of the children who were living indoors for months at a time. In 1934 Dr Crockatt introduced the use of Infra-Red lamps. Bigger and better X-ray machines were needed, but the key to the treatment of the TB cases were the plaster

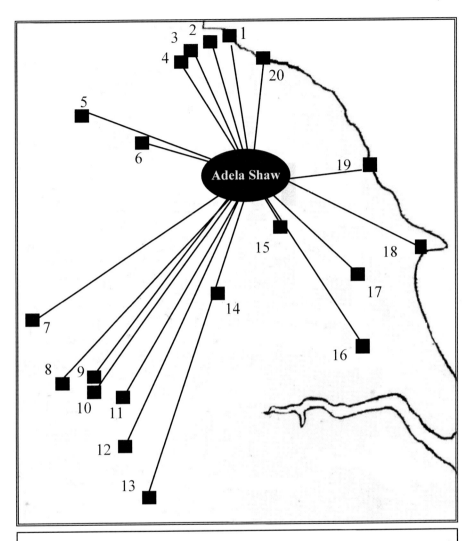

■ Orthopaedic clinics served by the Adela Shaw Hospital in 1946

1	Redcar	8	Brighouse	15	Malton
2	South Bank	9	Batley	16	Beverley
3	Middlesbrough	10	Dewsbury	17	Driffield
4	Thornaby	11	Wakefield	18	Bridlington
5	Richmond	12	Barnsley	19	Scarborough
6	Northallerton	13	Rotherham	20	Carlin How
7	Keighley	14	York		

frames and the year round open wards that housed the children. In 1931 the hospital board recommended that only tuberculin tested/certified milk was to be used for the children – obvious though this may seem to us this was a very forward thinking step. The Bovine TB from which the children were suffering was caught through infected milk. In the 1930s around 40% of all dairy cattle had Bovine TB*and this infection when contracted through drinking the raw milk, settled in the joints. Incredible as it may sound now the children were kept exposed to the fresh air day and night, on open veranda-style wards whilst the joints of affected limbs were kept open using metal frames or supports and plaster casts prevented movement. This meant the children were immobilised for months if not years but if caught early enough their prognosis was good. Those who did not have TB were kept on the other side of the wards, but no doubt they too got the benefit of the fresh air albeit in smaller doses. On average 130 surgical operations were being done each year and the average death rate was around one, mostly as a result of spinal TB.

Beds and children out on the veranda of the West Riding ward of the Hospital

Hand in hand with the operations and nursing care received on the wards, the hospital developed a network of aftercare clinics which meant children could be sent home earlier and benefit from continuing treatment in the form of exercises, manipulations and massage. The first clinics were established in York, Leeds, Wakefield, Rotherham, Scarborough and Middlesbrough and by 1929 there were 13 clinics in total. These clinics offered 21 sessions per month with an average of 18 patients at each clinic.

* source - DEFRA website

Such a demanding workload meant increased staffing levels and the After-Care Sister and radiologist Miss E S Braemer, based at Kirbymoorside, required transport. To this end the board agreed to the purchase of a small Austin 7 car at a cost of £135 in 1929, for the use of Matron and another Austin car purchased for Miss Braemer and her colleague, who was recruited to assist her in 1944. After seven years' service (1946) it had done 100,000 miles. By the end of WWII there were 21 clinics covering the North East and West Riding; many were funded by the local health authorities that also had to defray the staffing costs which were a heavy burden for the hospital to carry. However Dr Crockatt firmly believed that continuous care was the only way forward. Children could be monitored and if things began to deteriorate he was in a position to take immediate action. It was also a lifeline for families to get access to Dr Crockatt and his team in areas that they would never otherwise have encountered. The next big challenge facing the Yorkshire Children's Orthopaedic Hospital was to come in 1939 with the outbreak of the Second World War.

With the outbreak of hostilities the hospital came under the direction of the Government. Beds were made available for emergency medical cases and some of the children were moved to Welburn Hall to free up two wards for treatment of soldiers; the Shaw family once again had given over their home for the war effort. The local Women's Institutes in the North Riding sent in donations of feather stuffing for the soldiers' pillows. About 70 beds were bought to fit out the annexe and nursing staff moved to tend the children. The recreation room was turned into an emergency ward for soldiers and remained as a ward until 1942, when it became apparent that the hospital could cope with the existing facilities. The need for staff outstripped those coming forward and the Red Cross and Civil Nursing Reserves were brought in to help. The number of beds rose from 124 to 250 and 1940 saw a surge of emergency medical cases as a result of the Dunkirk evacuations. The Ministry of Health upgraded the hospital to a Fracture 'A' Clinic – dealing with long-term recovery cases - but it was allowed to continue to take in children. Such was the recognition of the value of the hospital's non-military duties. Lord Feversham offered his home, Nawton Towers, as another annexe and on 24 October 1941 the hospital sent the first of 24 child patients, those who did not need teaching instruction. The remote location some six miles away made recruiting staff even more of a challenge but the hospital again made it possible, through the ruthless efficiency and determination of

Matron Poole and Sister D Gray who ran this remote annexe from 1943. Temporary staff were recruited as the men such as Mr Blenkhorn, the clerk, were called up to do military service. Ms Clewes had to take over his post, although the hospital were legally obliged to hold a post open for him on his return, an offer he took up after the war.

With more staff, the issue of lodgings again became a problem. In 1942 Mr H Rivis offered the hospital first option on the purchase of a three-bed house in Castlegate [now called Norfolk House]. After an inspection, the property was bought by the hospital at a cost of £870; this house would then be rented out to the secretary for a fee of £50 per year. The secretary to benefit from the new house would be Mr Ronald Simpson. He joined the hospital staff in 1943 from the Stockton & Thornaby Hospital at a salary of £400 pa and would stay there for years to come.

Left: Eric Blenkhorn Right: Ronald Simpson

It was at the beginning of Second World War that the hospital changed its name; in September 1940 the Board agreed to apply for incorporation under the Companies Act of 1929. A new constitution was formulated and all paperwork completed by March 1941. In recognition of Mrs Shaw's dedication to the hospital The Adela Shaw Orthopaedic Hospital came into being. Even then the authorities were beginning to note that the average age of the population was rising and whilst the hospital's primary role would continue to be the treatment of children, they should also accept adult cases in need of their specialist care.

In October 1940 as part of a national campaign, the hospital took in 125 chronic sick cases from cities, which were suffering heavy damage due to the Blitz. These people were accommodated in the emergency ward created from the recreation room. One such group of patients came to the hospital from a Catholic Care Home in London. Sadly many of these elderly women did not survive long and were buried in All Saints churchyard far from their families. The dates given relate to the church's burial register.

1. **Mary Ann Holt** *83 years*   29 Nov 1940
2. **Anna Nabel** *82 years*   13 Dec 1940

3.   **Rose Phillips** *79 years*   16 Dec 1940
4.   **Ellen Bromley** *92 years*   24 Dec 1940
5.   **Margaret Smith** *86 years*   10 Jan 1941
6.   **Louisa Rigby** (otherwise **Everard**) *64 years*   10 Jan 1941
7.   **Annie Lilley** *76 years*   15 Jan 1941
8.   **Elizabeth Jane Tisdell** *84 years*   24 Jan 1941
9.   **Eliza A Pike** *90 years*   24 Jan 1941
10. **Mary Deelen** *83 years*   14 Feb 1941
11. **Eliza Elizabeth Kemp** *67 years*   14 Mar 1941
12. **Eliza Ann Bangor** *90 years*   18 Mar 1941
13. **Rosina E White** *73 years*   7 July 1941
14. **Elizabeth Cornforth** *84 years*   25 July 1941

Of the 125 cases sent to Kirbymoorside in 1940, 26 died, 69 returned home and 30 remained by 1942. The doctors were unhappy that these people had not been moved as the ward they were in was only meant to be a temporary measure. After pressure from the Board to the authorities in Whitehall, they were all finally transferred to the Hemlington Hospital in Middlesbrough in January 1943.

Isolation Block
Yorkshire County Orthopædic Hospital. Kirbymoorside
Hayes   592

On 23 June 1942 the hospital was visited again by HRH Princess Mary, who had opened the hospital in 1925. She toured the wards, met the children and spoke with the soldiers recuperating on the two wards which had been set aside for their use.

The D-Day landings and arrival of over 300 soldiers in 1944 put a great deal of strain on the hospital and its staff again; the Board expressed their thanks for the dedication and commitment of all those who kept the hospital going. Additional duties such as fire watching were done by the staff volunteers on a rota basis and protective measures such as earthen banks designed to absorb impact in case of bombing had to be built by the staff on site. The pressure of work took its toil as equipment began to fail; the floors and supports already weakened had to be strengthened, the drains and water supplies struggled to cope and even in the kitchen equipment needed renewing - an industrial Kelvinator refrigerator had to be purchased at a cost of £135. The workload had its effect on the staff. Mr Walker, their ambulance driver, retired due to ill health after 17

Matron Poole (seated) and her staff, including Sister Bedwell seated in the middle.

years service. Mr John W Marflitt from the laundry also was forced to retire through sickness in 1946 and died the following year aged 71 years. Miss Braemer, the after care sister, also succumbed to illness and at the end of the war Matron Poole who had worked at the hospital from the very beginning could not continue. Her health had suffered and also being beyond retirement age, she gave in her notice and left on 31 January 1946. In recognition of her 20 years at the hospital the Board agreed to an extra £1 per year on top of her annual pension of £108 and also paid her removal costs of £33; as they were reminded she had provided all her own furniture. Her replacement was to be Matron Gertrude Bedwell, herself one of the first nurses at the hospital in 1926; she had taken charge of the Welburn Hall annexe and was in turn replaced by Matron Lillie.

In April 1945 the annexes at Nawton Towers and Welburn were closed and by 1946 the last of the soldiers had left the site. It was at this stage that Dr Crockatt came up with the idea of using Welburn Hall as a home for the children who did not need to be in hospital. Under the new Education Act the Ministry of Education had a duty to make provision for the handicapped pupils at the hospital. In May 1945 Dr Crockatt had spoken to Major Shaw and he had intimated that the Hall could be leased for use as a home, independent of the hospital in terms of administration and teaching but still drawing on the expertise of the doctors at Kirbymoorside. This project took some time to become reality but in 1951 Welburn Hall Boarding School opened its doors.

Matron Bedwell with Derek Davis on Babies' Ward IV

The post war period brought its own problems. There was still a shortage of materials, goods and manpower. A minute recorded in 1946 shows the hospital committee, struggling to find sufficient staff wrote, to Whitehall requesting **"an allocation of four displaced persons from the continent to assist in the kitchens etc."** The porter from the Nawton Towers annexe, Mr Stanton, was retained and taken on to work at the Kirbymoorside site. In 1946 Dr Crockatt noted that patients could not be discharged because of a lack of boots so an application had to be made to the Board of Trade for a float of 200 clothing coupons to free up beds. Mr Ward of Pickering and Mr Hutchinson of Huddersfield organised local dances for the hospital funds on 25 January 1947 in Pickering and Nawton respectively. Costs of caring for these patients had risen to £51 9s 9d by 1945 and the hospital had 209 beds. In 1948 the hospital finally became part of the National Health Service. It became part of a group serving the residents of Malton, Whitby and Bridlington, with the centre being at Scarborough. At the winding up meeting sincere thanks were paid to Adela Shaw who had devoted 23 years' service to the hospital.

Another result of the arrival of the NHS was the demise of the home-nurse. Set up in April 1909 the idea around this post was to provide care at home for those in need of nursing. Miss Judson was appointed to cover Kirbymoorside and Kirkdale and this was one of the first nursing associations in the North Riding. However this task was taken on by the NHS and she retired after 37 years' service to the community.

The next section deals with the memories and accounts of a few involved in various aspects of hospital life. Whilst we have tried to check as much detail as possible, as with any recollection, it is by its very nature imperfect and subjective. However they help us see the hospital in a more colourful and human way, and these snapshots help bring the story to life. The surnames given are maiden names: any later married names are in [ ].

The life of the hospital

Matron Christine M Lillie took up this key post in the running of the hospital in 1949. The following extracts are taken from the entries in her log book, which she kept on a monthly basis and give us an insight into the life that was going on around the patients. She was responsible for the management of not only the patients, the nursing staff and the auxiliary staff but also greeting visitors and acting as the link between the Committee managing the hospital and her staff who were running it. It was a job which required total commitment and was a vocation which she fulfilled until 19 February 1966 when she retired.

Matron Lillie

Her first entry on 31 August 1949 shows one matron, one home sister, one housekeeping sister, one sister tutor, one theatre sister, four ward sisters, one night sister and 28 student nurses. With four wards of patients to care for, she had to ensure enough staff was on duty to cover all the stations. Her log book lists all the events which conspired against her in the forms of illness, accidents and marriages, and show that it was a constant juggling act to ensure the patients did not suffer.

In February 1950 she records an outbreak of chickenpox amongst the children. Unlike today where chickenpox is seen as something to be caught as early as possible, in an orthopaedic hospital in early 1950 this was a real concern for the staff. Children had to be put into isolation to try to prevent the illness spreading to those already immobilised or with weakened health. The bedding had to be kept separate whilst it was cleaned and the staff were also at risk of catching chickenpox, which meant they could not care for the children. Matron Lillie's frustration with the situation is highlighted in a problem with the laundry equipment. She notes that they did not have a separate wash house, disinfecting tank, hydro extractor or autoclave to disinfect and sterilise the bedding which included mattresses. No visitors were allowed on site whilst the outbreak was contained and this lasted for two months. In May 1951 Matron noted that they were able to purchase a steam press which improved things, as it also increased the heating in the drying room.

The nurses who were trained and were employed as sisters were expected to leave if they were to be married; the concept of married women in this care profession was not a common one until they had started their families and they could then return to work if they were able to juggle home life and work life. There were no special allowances made in those days for a working mum

The bulk of Matron's resignations came from the nurses, who very often were aged 16 -18 years and had come into the hospital to train in child orthopaedics until they were old enough to take their general training certificate as a nurse. The nurses had to take exams on a regular basis, sometimes at the hospital and other times they would travel as far afield as Pinderfields Hospital in Wakefield and the Midlands - often travelling in the hospital's ambulance! When the nurses passed or decided they were not cut out for nursing, the logbook was noted and the task of recruiting new staff continued. Nurses moved onto the bigger hospitals in Edinburgh, Nottingham, Middlesbrough and Leeds where they took another three years to train to become qualified. Some would then return to Kirkbymoorside as sisters. Matron also noted those of her nurses who won prizes in the exams and one nurse, Nurse Swallow, was awarded £5 in books for being placed first out of 196 candidates, who came from England and Scotland. When she left to continue her training in Leeds, the committee awarded her another £2 2/- to be spent on books. One other nurse who stood out for Matron Lillie was Nurse Marie Shipley who trained at The Adela Shaw and obtained her Orthopaedic Nursing Certificate. She went on to do her general training in York Hospital and was presented with a gold medal as Best Nurse of the Year in 1965. Nurse Shipley had previously been a patient at The Adela Shaw as a child, undergoing a hip operation. Matron arranged for a telegram to be sent from all the staff at the hospital, congratulating her on her achievement. Those who did not succeed or needed to re-sit their exams were also recorded by Matron.

For Matron, the care of these nurses was a major part of her work. She records how they were treated and what issues they faced. She had to deal with them as a parent would, deal not only with their worries, but also with the troubles which are inevitable with teenagers. At one point she had 31 student nurses, and was in desperate need of more rooms:

"We have a total of 45 bedrooms occupied by nursing and domestic staff – the number of people sleeping in the hospital is as follows:

Administrative staff – 8   Staff Nurses - 3
Student Nurses - 31   Resident Maids – 8
Physiotherapists – 1

That is 51 for 45 bedrooms. I wish to draw attention to the fact that six of these rooms are being used as double rooms. For this purpose, they are much too small; and I regret very much having to do this. In order to accommodate the requisite number of staff we require at the very least 12 more rooms preferably 15, 16 if we can have more domestic staff sleeping in."

Child patient Susan Doran in 1949

With such numbers of young girls in the hospital it was essential that they had an outlet for their energies and their free time was also the concern of the Matron. She noted how and where they spent their leisure time. For instance one of the first outings noted by Matron Lillie in August 1949 was that **"a small party of nurses and Matron participated in a bramble hunt with a picnic tea. The outing was very successful"**. This was a regular event with other bramble hunts often detailing Dr Adamson taking the girls out in her car to places such as Douthwaite Hall by kind invitation of Mrs Fuller. It was not always brambles that were collected; in May 1950 the nurses collected enough mushrooms on a mushroom hunt to feed all the staff the next morning. Another regular trip for the staff was to the open air theatre at Scarborough with transport provided courtesy of the committee. This continued for many years and was a welcome escape from in-house entertainment. Matron notes that the doctors were the main support for all these additional activities, with Dr

Joan Rogers [Brockett] , back home with her mum Edith, after her first stay in The Adela Shaw Hospital aged four years. The pram and dolls were given to her in 1949 as a present for being good. Joan returned again at age nine for another leg operation.

Above : Nurse Nora Barwick [Richardson] with the young sportsmen of Ward II in the late 1940s.

Below: Ivy Charlton [Watson] and the girls of Ward III out in the fresh air.

Above : Nurse Ruth Wood from Ebberston who was on Ward IV with Sister Easton in 1949; seen here enjoying the sunshine at the hospital with her small charges.

Crockatt coaching dramatics as well as playing music to allow the nurses to learn country dancing.

In October 1949 there was a meeting to discuss the formation of a recreation club – something which was much needed. Activities which took place were as follows:

> **"We have had sewing evenings, when Dr K Adamson very kindly displayed her work, and offered assistance with tapestry and fancy work in general. The staff are all very keen to learn new stitches, Dr Crockatt, very generously attended the badminton evenings and gave tuition which was very much appreciated. Table tennis has also been played. On 31 October we had a fancy dress dance. After the judging of the costumes, which was done by Dr and Mrs Crockatt and Dr Adamson; games and dancing followed."**

Weekly dancing classes were also arranged for the nurses, with Mrs Jackson teaching old time dancing; all very suitable pursuits for young ladies. However these more old-fashioned interests faded with time.

With ever-changing times the types of activities arranged by the Matron and other staff for the girls changed too. In 1950 the records which had previously provided the music had been replaced by a band. The nurses were beginning to give concerts and perform plays for the rest of the hospital. Trips to York, to see the mystery plays and to Stockton to see the musical *"Maid of the Mountain"* are recorded as were regular outings to the pantomimes at Pickering and Malton. Whatever was available to see or do in the area Matron and the clerical staff arranged for her nurses to go there, . As time went by the hospital opened its doors to the local community and dances became a regular event with good suppers to follow. In 1949 the staff asked if their relatives could be allowed to see the Christmas decorations – which Matron allowed and this led to a regular annual Open Day for family and friends to see the girls at work; always with tea to follow - hospitality was a by-word for Matron, as she felt this reflected on her personally.

Considering the large numbers of young teenage girls under her care, the problems noted by Matron Lillie are remarkably few in comparison to today's world. Whilst she had an overview of what they did she was not involved to a great extent; the girls were good at staying under her radar for the majority of the time. However one nurse did make it into the log book with her behaviour and Matron's displeasure is clear to see following a dance at the recreation room on the 3 March 1953:

"Nurse D did not return to the nurses' home, when the above dance finished at 1am. She was still not in her room when the night sister called again at 2am. The home doors were locked. When sister called again after 2am Nurse was in bed and appeared to be asleep. When I asked Nurse the following morning how she got into her room, she said through the sitting room window. She was in the hospital grounds with her boyfriend until 2am. After considering this very carefully, also the reaction on the student nurses, as regards discipline in this hospital, I suggested to Nurse D it would be better if she resigned from her post here as a student nurse. She did not hand her resignation in, and came to me on Monday morning, and stated she was not handing in her resignation, as she was very happy here and liked her work, and furthermore she had signed the application form in order to sit the preliminary orthopaedic examinations in May.

I told Nurse it was at least three years since anyone had behaved in this way previously; quite briskly she informed me, it was not. She knew of someone else; but she would not give anyone away. (This was the first intimation I had of the latter)"

Such a serious challenge to her authority over the hospital and its staff could not be allowed. Not only was this disruptive to the existing students, but as she tells us, the parents of other potential student nurses were always concerned as to who would be living at the hospital and how well cared for their 16 year old daughters would be. If parents did not feel that Matron was in control and could act in loco parentis then the reputation of the hospital would suffer and applicants would go elsewhere. Matron Lillie referred this to the Committee and asked for their consideration. The Committee interviewed Nurse D in connection with this incident and after further problems with obeying the hospital rules Nurse D failed her exam and was asked by the Committee to resign - which she did. It was not only being caught out of hours that brought the nurses to Matron's attention. In 1955 a nurse, no doubt in preparation for one of the many successful dances at the hospital, left an iron on in the Nurses' sitting room which led to a small fire which was put out by one of the outside staff who saw the smoke. The floors being wooden and well worn were damaged and so Matron had to be informed – however the nurse dealt with Matron in a very different way :

"the nurse responsible for this, has been most concerned about this accident and has presented her apologies, and sincere regret of the whole incident."

No further action was taken other than raising a question as to whether irons would be banned from the sitting room in future.

Matron also had deputations from the more senior staff, who brought their complaints regarding the food and the conditions in the nurses' home, which was too cold for comfort. All these issues Matron Lillie had to act upon. In 1958 Matron Lillie received a request from the staff to change the colour of the ward sisters' uniform from navy blue to maroon with belts to match and brown shoes which the sisters would buy themselves. Matron had to approach the Committee and get their approval, which she succeeded in doing. Many of her other requests were constant pleas for the hospital to be kept decorated and bright and cheery for the patients; a never ending battle against the age of the site and buildings on it.

As Matron she was also responsible for all visitors to her hospital and as always meticulous records were kept. Here are a few of the foreign visitors who over the years came to see the work and children of The Adela Shaw Hospital:

- **Danish Cadets with British Red Cross – August 1949**
- **10 teachers from Iraq – August 1952**
- **German student engineer – August 1952**

- Antiguan Junior Red Cross - June 1953
- Cypriot teachers – November 1953 and Sept 1955, 1956
- Seven lady broadcasters from the Gold Coast – Sept 1954
- New Zealand Welfare Nurses – January 1959
- Somali teachers – June 1962
- Auxiliaries from West Indies and Trinidad - 1962

Visiting Cypriot Teachers in 1954 greeted by Miss Rippon (1) and Matron Lillie (2)

All these guests had to be escorted and entertained and of course served with tea.

Matron Lillie also tells us who were regular visitors and supporters of the hospital. Any reader of her log will be struck by the generosity of the public from all over England and the world, such was the reputation of the hospital. Alongside the technical and specialist support staff, the log book lists donations from local organisations and residents alike. Harvest festival gifts were given each year by the local churches and chapels and all were gratefully received by the staff and children. Books and comics came for the children, newspapers organised collections and donated larger items such as a table tennis table. Shortly after the war in 1949 Matron's log lists the delivery of gift parcels from the American Roman Catholic Society which were distributed among the patients by the Red Cross Society. Interestingly 200lb of rice was also received via the Director of Commonwealth Gift Fund from Mr and Mrs Gray, New Orleans. The Australian Junior Red

Cross sent 120 packets of boiled sweets in 1950 and the miners at Ling, Guisborough sent a stick of rock weighing 70lb. Mr Wilson and Mr Summerville of York, were annual donators of Easter eggs and Christmas gifts for the youngsters.

Matron Lillie tells us that at Christmas 1950 the hospital received a bumper delivery of goods:

"This year people have been exceedingly kind to the children and I have much pleasure in recording the following to be used for Xmas festivities:

Mr J B Foster East Field, North Cave, Brough – handmade waggons and furniture

Mr A E Robson, Scalby Mills Scarborough – books and toys

Miss K Miller, Ruswarp Whitby – books and toys

Miss Crossland Hutton-le-Hole – dolls, scrapbooks, games

Rev. Patrick & Children Slingsby Church – books, toys "Gift Sunday"

The Misses Richards, 9 Meadvale East Cayton – hand-knitted woollies for babies

Miss Barker 1st Guides Co. Grosmont – Hand-knitted blanket

Mr Charlton Scout master Middlesbrough Scouts – 1 large Christmas cake

Mr Frank White Ltd, Oratory St Mary Devon – 1 large Christmas cake

Snainton Church Gift Sunday – toys and books

Riccall Women's Institute – hand-knitted garments for babies, matinee coats and vests

Kirkdale Gift Sunday – books, toys and games

INL Working Men's Club York – bag of fruit, sweets and a game for each child, also fruit for nursing staff.

I understand that three [members] of the above now living in the Poor's House clubbed together and bought a beautiful basket of fruit for the children here.

Major and Mrs J Shaw – Christmas trees

Mr Barker, York father of a patient by having dances whist drives and concert raised £16 17s 6d. He also sent individual parcels to several of the children.

Mr Rich sent £2 2s 0d

Scout master and Scouts Cleckheaton, by the boys' own efforts, - £6 0s 0d

Mr Giles - £8 14s 6d

Members of the Riccall's Women's Institute - £2 2s 0d"

Some of the children were in need of clothing, coming from poorer backgrounds than others and here too Matron notes that the public were very good at providing whatever the children needed; even down to old prams and used cricket bats for the children to use. Miss Baldwin, of Sinnington, used to provide theatre socks for the children on a regular basis. Money raised by the Kirkbymoorside Darts League (£13) was donated to buy clothing or anything necessary for needy children.

In June 1953 in preparation for the Queen's coronation Mrs Adela Shaw presented the children with a television set, which was soon to be followed by another donated by the Muffin Club. This no doubt eased the competition between the children as to who could watch what, but when the new TV channel ITV came into being it was a matter for discussion by the Committee as to whether it would be suitable viewing for the children. For many children who were not able to get out on the organised trips this provided an invaluable link to the outside world and lessened their isolation. The radio was also very popular and the children on the wards were even gifted a tropical fish tank, complete with fish and a budgerigar in a cage.

Matron Lillie's commitment to the Red Cross should also be mentioned, as her log details her interest in training others. She asked that lectures could be held on site in the Recreation Room and these continued throughout her years at the hospital. She also had Red Cross members into the hospital to do training; in 1953 Mrs Rickaby and Mrs Fryer were the first to be mentioned in the log to do their 48 hours and complete their hospital nursing certificates. She also gave lectures herself to various local groups and took examinations with Dr Adamson and Miss Bedwell (retired matron). Although she does not make much of it in her log, Matron Lillie was invited to attend the examination centre for nurses at Heatherwood Orthopaedic Hospital, Ascot in Berkshire as an examiner. This was an honour and recognition of her abilities and commitment to her work.

Godfrey Woof is another name synonymous with The Adela Shaw Hospital. From the opening of the splint shop in 1931 until its closure, Godfrey was a familiar face to all those who needed specialist braces or splints. At the very start of the hospital's life all equipment for the children came from Oswestry which was the centre for making supports and callipers; there ex-servicemen were trained in adapting splints for use in hospitals. However Dr Crockatt felt that the hospital should provide their own, as all too often the items did not fit and had to be altered, taking up precious time and money. So in September 1930 a specialist workshop was formed staffed by two men, both of whom had trained at Oswestry - Mr Fields who was the metal worker and Mr Woof who made the leather supports. Godfrey had suffered from polio as a child and wore a calliper himself; he would come to work in an invalid carriage. An early newspaper report on the tenth anniversary of the hospital gives a brief glimpse into those first few years:

Above: Godfrey Woof

"An interesting branch of the hospital work was seen in the splint and instrument room. Here I found Mr WC Fields making all kind of splints, callipers and supports, while Mr G Woof made the leather work, boots and padding. Mr Woof told me that he makes hundreds of pairs of boots yearly quite apart from the hospital patients' requirements, constructing a last from the measurements of the foot itself.

"One thing I was particularly interested in was a jacket which was being made to fit the back of a young girl, to support the spine. A plaster cast had been taken of the whole back and skull. This was converted into the positive and allowed to dry. A linen-like material called certalmid was then pasted onto the cast, layer by layer until a good thickness had been obtained, after which the plaster was chipped away leaving a perfect jacket. This, of course, would be finished off, reinforced and varnished."

Above: Godfrey in the splint shop

Over the years the specialism of the unit grew and the number of men employed increased. In 1936 they took on their first assistant Mr Edward Gee who had already worked down in Oswestry. When he left others soon followed. Mr Jackie Baxter became an apprentice metal worker in 1940 and trained with Mr Field. A former patient Ernest Ellwood was taken on as an apprentice, aged 14½ years, in 1941 and he was trained by Mr Woof. Mr W Smith joined the team in 1942 having already done a four-year apprenticeship in leatherwork at Manfield Orthopaedic Hospital. From a total of 273 supplied appliances and 75 repairs in 1931 the output of the splint shop had risen to 2,100 items by 1946. Equipment ordered by the doctors in the morning was usually made and fitted by the afternoon.

The workshop was at the top of the site and is remembered by many of the former staff as a world of its own. Names associated with it include Paddy Cresswell from Ireland, Tom Frisby, Jackie Baxter, Tom Hammond, Freddie Harrison and George [Podge] Fenwick, another who was lame in one leg and rode a specially adapted bike. Local resident **Robert [Bob] Pettit** recalls working in the workshop from 1949 when he was 15 years old. On his first day he went from Gillamoor down to Kirkby on his bike, wearing short trousers, and when he got to the workshop Jackie Baxter said "We'll have to get you kitted out better than that" and gave him a pair of his old overalls. Starting on a salary of 15 shillings, he worked under Jackie and did a lot of fetching and carrying up and down the site. He brought the milk up from the kitchens for the daily allowance and brought boots to and from the wards.

Left to Right: Paddy Cresswell, Jackie Baxter, Freddie Harrison, Godfrey Woof, Tom Frisby, Ron Porritt

He remembers Dr Crockatt working together with Godfrey Woof in the office at the workshop to design and make specialist items. Godfrey did the measuring up and the final fittings. This design would then be passed onto Jackie and Bob to make and then to the other side of the workshop for any leatherwork to be added before it was tried out by the patient. The workshop made and fitted the pulleys for the beds and generally anything that was needed. They supplied not only the Kirkby patients but also Malton and the outlying hospitals. He remembers a jovial atmosphere with Godfrey leading the way with the practical jokes. One incident he remembers vividly involved himself, an errand onto Ward III, several nurses and a pot of iodine. Another incident which we can relate involved a barrel that the workshop crew had acquired for a tombola at Christmas time. Attached to the barrel was a label telling them to make sure it was washed out as it contained the remnants of some vintage port. Not wanting to waste it, Godfrey Woof bottled what was left and it was described by all as "a bit of good stuff". Everyone sampled it, with one worker from the laundry being especially susceptible to its strength. Not wishing to lose the opportunity for a great prank, this lady was then bundled into a laundry hamper and put onto the cart driven by Jim

Clark who was headed for the railway station. They had planned to stop her before she had gone very far; unfortunately Mr Ron Simpson the secretary heard her calls for help and got to the hamper before they did. Needless to say they got into trouble for that one.

Another tale involved the stove in the workshop. One visitor regularly came in to see them and rattled the stove with the poker, whether it needed it or not. To put a stop to this irritating habit, the men heated the poker and put it back hot end up. His next visit was the last time he rattled the stove.

Joking apart, the workshop staff were all committed to the hospital in many ways and Matron Lillie regularly noted the things they did for the children. They were responsible for helping arrange the scenery for the concerts and took part in them as well. Every year they would put on a firework display for the children and arranged dances and games for staff and visitors alike. At Christmas the workshop built a sleigh and acquired Father Christmas and reindeer outfits. The secretary Mr Simpson, Dr Crockatt and later Mr Welford played the part of Santa and the workshop men filled the other roles. All this made for a family atmosphere and one which Bob had hoped to return to following his National Service in 1952; however this wasn't possible and this is something he still regrets.

Some of the others employed in and around the workshop remembered were Septimus Dawson who was in charge of the boilers; his boiler house was a popular place for a cup of tea and a chat during the colder months. Mr Metcalfe was in charge of outside repairs, Jack Magson and Harry Owston worked in the grounds with Arthur Masterman, Mr Stockdale and Fred Jackson.

Dorothy Magson [Brand] left work in the kitchens at the Work House in Dale End in 1949 and started at the hospital as a maid in the classrooms and isolation ward. The cook in charge of the hospital kitchen was Mrs Flora Charlton and the undercook was Mrs Richardson, both of whom had been there for many years. When Mrs Charlton resigned in 1950 Dorothy [Do] moved over to help out, having cooked previously. However Mrs Richardson followed with her resignation and Do was left to run the kitchens. She was joined by Miss Dorothy Coggill on 4 December 1950. Miss Coggill was the daughter of the parson at Ebberston and had gained a diploma in Good

Housekeeping in London. Alongside them they had three German girls working in the kitchens, part of the allocation of displaced persons that Lillie had sought. Do remember everyone was fascinated with these Germans in the kitchen - Ilsa and Charlotte Liepera [sic] and later Herta Purche. Whenever they went out shopping they would buy clothes to send home to Germany. They also enjoying knitting, but used round needles and worked in the opposite direction to the English knitters.

Kitchen staff shifts started one week at 6.30 am till dinnertime then from 5 pm -7.30 pm to cook suppers, whilst the following week the shift began at 8 am. Meals were prepared for the whole hospital, apart from Matron's breakfast which was prepared by her maid, Vera Smith [Cook]. All other meals were collected by trolley by the ward maids and the nursing staff would eat in their dining room. Meals were cooked en masse. Supplies were allocated by Sister Carrick. She would dispense dry goods such as tea coffee sugar etc into baskets, brought by the ward maids who waited outside her office. She also gave the kitchen staff their ingredients and supplies, sufficient for the amount of meals to be cooked. When Sister Carrick left Miss Coggill took over the allocation of supplies. Matron Lillie is remembered as tall and strict but very nice. All the staff knew that Matron did not tolerate talking and everyone had to be busy when she did her rounds.

Meals were simple - often meat and vegetables such as braised steak and onions and Sunday roasts and always fish on Fridays. An enormous toaster providing the wards with breakfast, two Aga cookers stood back to back they used a large urn, a deep fat fryer for fish and an industrial size food mixer. All along one end there were enormous cupboards and drawers as well as two large tables to work at. Most of the vegetables and potatoes were stored outside in a shed. Christmas dinners was done on a rota basis with the nursing staff waiting on the kitchen staff for their dinners. At Christmas Matron would give the kitchen and other staff presents whilst the nursing staff sang carols and went round the wards with candles.

Others remembered as working there over the years include Doreen Windress, Molly Tateson, who was deaf and dumb, Annie, Betty and Hannah Kent, Mary Meek with Lois Bowes [Rex] assisting when not in the laundry. Mrs Elsie Prattley was in charge of the laundry with Tilly Dowkes, Beatie Ezard, Bertha Hepton [Smith], Peggy Kent working there over the years. Mr Dawson also dealt with the heavy lifting. The laundry not only did the washing for the Kirkby site but also sent laundry to Malton by train, with the hampers being transferred on horse and cart by Jim Clark, one of the older workers at the site. The two ladies in the sewing room which was opposite the kitchens, were Mrs Vinnie Ford and Milly Hewitt. All staff uniforms were repaired, named and altered on site, aprons, sheets and screens also came from the sewing room, as did all the curtains for the wards and nurses' home. Doris Deighton and Joan Bell cleaned in the Nurses Home,Freda Smith and Ethel Ford waited on in the dining room. Do's aunt, Julie Magson, used to help out in the kitchens.

Francis Rex worked as maid on Ward III, Miss Coates on Ward I, Molly Moody on Ward II, Mrs Fryer on Ward IV. Mrs Wardle and Mrs Garbutt from Dale End worked as orderlies on a night. The ward maids were responsible for the cleaning of their own particular ward, as well as collecting the daily rations from the store's Sister. They collected the meals on trolleys and helped with mealtimes. Once delivered to the wards, these meals were transferred to warming cupboards until the nurses were ready to serve the patients. The maids were very proud of their work and every so often the ward maids would concentrate on a ward and give it a deep clean. All the wooden floors had to be cleaned between the crevices with a painter scraper to get all the dust out. The corridors were wooden with rubber matting along the centre. The wooden parts had to be polished every day; with Mrs Ted Sherwood cleaning the corridors and Mrs Jos Frank [Joseph] who wielded a huge heavy polishing bumper and would swing it from one hand to another. The cleanliness of the hospital was paramount and it took a lot of hard work by the staff to keep the old buildings up to standard. When the dust became a problem the maids would scatter wet tea leaves onto the boards to sleck the dust, before sweeping them all up.

Doreen Windress [Pettitt] had started work at the hospital in 1954 and she remembers her first day, walking from Gillamoor in black plimsolls at the age of 15. These black plimsolls were also noticed by Do who met her on her first day in the kitchens. Kitchen staff wore a uniform which was green and white with a cap. Each day a huge Belfast sink of potatoes had to be peeled ready for the next day and the cooked potatoes were mashed in huge aluminium coppers. The kitchen served everyone with breakfast, dinner, afternoon teas and supper, and the cakes had to be baked every morning. Miss Coggill used to mix the ingredients for the cakes in a huge mixer before giving it a final stir with her arm to make sure the bottom was mixed properly. All the work surfaces and the kitchen floors had to be washed and scrubbed every day. Doreen lived in at the staff quarters and this meant she was subject to the same discipline as the nurses. On one occasion she hadn't made her bed properly, with the hospital corners, and Sister Sinclair, Deputy Matron, on her rounds decided it wasn't good enough. All the bedclothes were unceremoniously removed and dumped on the floor so she had to start again. The local clergy were regular visitors to the site. Confirmation classes were held at the hospital for staff and patients and those who lived in had to get up early to fit in all these extras; once a month the staff had to get up at 6 am to go for communion in Matron's office.

Right : Charlie Metcalf along side one of the cream Adela Shaw ambulances which were garaged at the top of the site.

As previously mentioned the first real ambulances were donated by the Shaws and by the 1950s Nathaniel Parker was the ambulance driver of a very old pale cream ambulance, which was always kept meticulously clean by Mr Parker and Mr Metcalf. Nurses were taken to exams in it as well as collecting children from the outlying areas and taking them home at the end of the terms. Alan Rutter, Noel Lishman Cliff Weatherill, Barrie Wiley and Ken Ford were all drivers for the Ambulance Service and took the children to and from The Adela Shaw Hospital over the years.

This account of life in the hospital as a patient has kindly been supplied by **Mr Howard Youngs** who was a patient at the Adela Shaw between 1937 - 1940 and who now lives in Oakville Ontario, Canada.

"I was born in Redcar in 1935. When I was two and a half I slipped on the linoleum floor and fell on my

50

knee. It developed into osteomyelitis. I remember seeing a doctor in Redcar and then I was sent to the Children's Hospital in Kirbymoorside by ambulance for treatment. I was operated on by a Dr Crockatt. My leg was put into a splint and I wore this all the time I was there. I remember that I stayed in hospital until I was five years old.

Howard with his mum

"My mother and my father were only able to visit the first Saturday in every month. This was like Christmas as we all received presents. My mother had to take a bus from Redcar. My father made model airplanes and ships - this was one he sent to me. Sadly he died in 1944.

"When the war started, we were moved to an estate (I don't know the name) to make room for injured soldiers. I think that all the beds were put in a long room - such as a large dining hall. It was in the winter as we somehow were able to get a tin can - put some string on it throw it out of the window to get some snow.

51

"I remember going home once - but then taken back by ambulance to have another operation on my leg. The ward had shutters that were opened every morning and closed again at night. We had a teacher come in and try to school us but as we were all different ages it was just a general education.

"For fun we used to tie newspaper up and string it over the pipes that ran along the ceiling - we would then swing these back and forth. This way we were able to send stuff to some of the other beds.

"I can remember one time climbing out of bed and along with some other boys crawling out into the field that was alongside the hospital. The nurses were very good - but we all feared Sister and Matron. Our food was given to us in a steel bowl - mince, cabbage and mashed potatoes was the one meal I remember most. If something fell on the floor - I used my toes to pick it up! After being released I wore a calliper on my leg until I was about 11. I was able to walk again without a brace - but it left me with a weak leg - two inches shorter that the other one. It stopped me from doing any sports (cricket, football etc) and I still do not swim. It also affected my education - I was always behind in school - leaving school when I was 15. However - having said that - I have a very good life here in Canada and am grateful of the care I received from the hospital. My Mother often mentioned Dr. Crockatt - he was like a god to her. She told me he actually operated on himself "

Dr Crockatt was acutely aware of the impact of the hospital environment on the children and made a conscious decision not to wear a white coat and the children called him Mr Crockatt; he didn't want the children to be afraid of him. He always remarked how resilient the children were, when faced with the prospect of months, or even years, in a hospital environment away from their homes and families. One child was an in-patient for five years, flat on his back having treatment for TB of the spine. Eventually he was fit enough to be discharged home, but pleaded to stay for a further fortnight so that he could watch the annual cricket match in the field next to the hospital. Another tale told by Dr Crockatt involved a phone call he received one night during the war. He was advised that Welburn Hall had been attacked with incendiary bombs and he drove out to the Hall fearing the worst. On arrival he was met by the butler who was carefully carrying a fizzing incendiary bomb on a shovel. The bomb was tossed out of the door and the butler simply said "There – that's that one sorted!"

Stan Brough aged 80 years in 2009

Another child patient who arrived at The Adela Shaw by ambulance was **Stanley Brough**. He got polio in both feet at the age of six and couldn't walk. To try and help his parents tied a rope to the end of his iron bedstead to allow Stan pull himself upright. His doctor's advice was to tie balloons to the beams and to try to kick them, to get his mobility back. He still had to be pushed about in a large old fashioned wheel-chair by his dad until age 13. His father had heard about Dr Crockatt who ran a clinic at Northallerton and having examined him it was agreed that the hospital could help him. It was arranged for him to go to the hospital in June 1942, however his admission had to be delayed because this coincided with the visit by Princess Mary. The trip to Kirkbymoorside was in The Adela Shaw ambulance and he remembers they stopped at Wass Bank for their sandwiches at lunchtime. He was admitted into Ward I which had 16 beds in it, on the Thursday and had his operation on the Monday. Unfortunately the monthly visit was that weekend and his family could not get through to see him. This was as well as it was the first time away from home and he, like some of the other patients, felt really homesick. His legs were shaved by the nurses in preparation for the operation and afterwards he was put into plaster for six months. During his stay in hospital he saw the recovering soldiers in blue uniforms in Ward II but had little contact. He clearly remembers being concerned the bombers would come as the wooden huts looked like an army camp.

On the ward Sister Nancy Rickaby was in charge and Stan recalls her as a tall ginger-haired lady, who was married to a schoolteacher [Harry Rickaby]. Every ward had its entertainer and on Ward I it was a boy from Gateshead who would sing the George Formby song "*I'm leaning on the lamp-post…*" Ever inventive they found ways of adapting to life in bed and the schoolteacher Mr King would come into the ward two to three times a week. He would set angled boards onto the beds so they could be propped up and still do their reading and sums.

The ward doors were open all the time, if they were cold extra blankets appeared but these did not muffle the noise. From his bed Stan could see Dr Crockatt's house with a lawn in front and when the noise levels from the wards rose too high the telephone would ring and it would be Dr Crockatt telling the staff to keep them quiet. Meals were okay but one special treat sent in by his mum and dad was a box of fresh peas from home. After a month it was agreed that he could go home and Godfrey made some leather slip-on sandals to fit over his plaster casts. His father came to the hospital by taxi, but had to buy the necessary petrol coupons because of rationing.

By age 15 his condition had improved to such an extent that when he was offered an allotment he took it. He entered his allotment in the Dig for Victory campaign and was awarded a Certificate of Merit for his contribution to local food production. That in turn resulted in a job offer at Thirsk Hall as a gardener and despite his disability went on to work there in the gardens for another 43 years.

Thomas Baggley first came to The Adela Shaw Hospital from the New Street clinic in Barnsley at the age of 18 months, having contracted polio which affected his right foot and leg. He received treatment on and off for the next ten years and remembers "Mr" Crockatt as a great friend as well as a remarkable surgeon. He had to wear a calliper and special built-up boot which Godfrey made on Dr Crockatt's instructions. Each time he came in for another operation, his father had to carry him to the Barnsley clinic where he was met by Nurse Davis, who escorted him alone by train back to Kirkbymoorside. Once there his clothes were bagged up and the nurses bathed him in salt water to kill off any germs before putting him to bed. The hospital staff were warm and friendly, although his experience with the too salty porridge he was given has also never left him. His parents struggled to visit him because of the rationing of petrol and when his father did arrive he did not recognise his son, Tommy had been away for so long and had grown up. He also recalls the use of the pad over his nose and the liquid being poured onto it to put him to sleep and the struggle to come round afterwards. Each time he came into the hospital he had to bring his ration book. After the last operation in 1943 he awoke to see a German bomber flying low over the hospital and the glass roof gave him a perfect view of the plane. He felt the beds and the buildings shake as the bombs fell. All the children were taken to safety by the soldiers and army ambulances. Thankfully the bombs fell short, albeit by a two second delay on the part of the pilot, and the only damage done was to the fields behind the hospital. The last time he saw Dr Crockatt was at the clinic in Barnsley in 1947 when he was 17 years old and working as a cinema operator. The cost of the outpatient clinics run by Dr Crockatt were too high and treatment was transferred under the new NHS system to Barnsley Hospital. Three years later on 27 May 1950 he married his wife Lillian and they celebrate their 60th Anniversary this year (2010).

Tommy aged 80 - still wearing a three inch raised boot - the original design came from The Adela Shaw Hospital

The variety of people and groups who visited the hospital was truly amazing. Whenever possible the children would be taken out, the seaside being a popular location along with the local garden parties and picnics. They would be invited to events such as the Air Show at Topcliffe, Linton-on-Ouse, where the airmen constructed ramps to allow the children to see inside the planes. Groups of children were taken to the circus and shows and cinemas. At other times the entertainment would come to them. At times the hospital had seen animals from the zoo, puppet shows, concerts, acrobatic displays by the boys from Castle Howard Remand Home, bands, singers and dancing troupes. The children would have a weekly film show and daily TV and dedicated visitors from the Inner Wheel Club, for those children without anyone who could or would travel to see them. One special visitor came in a glider and landed in the neighbouring field much to the delight of the children.

Santa arrives by glider in December 1952. Allan Pratt was the test pilot for Slingsby Gliders and his arrival was reported in *The Yorkshire Post*

Other years he used the traditional method of arriving by reindeer and sleigh.

The following account was written by **Michael Newlove** from Hull who was a child patient from 1945 – 48:

"It was February 1945 when I was told I had to go into hospital, as I had TB in my right hip. I was taken by ambulance to York, and then put into the Adela Shaw Orthopaedic Hospital ambulance driven by Mr Metcalf, and taken to an old manor-type house, which was used as a hospital; I believe it was called Nawton Towers. I stayed there for a short time, and then I was transferred to The Adela Shaw Orthopaedic Hospital, Kirbymoorside. I can remember four other boys who were there at the same time - Michael Mawe, Michael Day, Ernie Noel and Ronny Abbey. Some nurses' names I can remember were Nurse Cox, Nurse Broderick, Nurse Thorne, Nurse Fox and Nurse Hardwick - I believe her family had buses in Scarborough.

"The girls' Ward III was behind the boys' Ward II and if we were lucky at Christmas some of us boys could go to see the girls. Ward I was for soldiers; they often had singing and entertainment that we could hear, as it was quite loud. We once had a children's radio programme broadcast from Ward II, I think it was Wilfred Pickles and a lady* playing the piano. There was a tall post with a long wire the length of the ward outside our ward to transmit the programme. We also had one or two film shows, mostly cowboys, or Will Hay comedies; all our beds would be put close together at one end of the ward. Some of us didn't see a lot of the film, but it was all exciting. We had an old wind-up gramophone with some old records, which we played over and over again. I can remember one of the tunes ended with the words "*...Ali Baba's camel won by half a camel's hair*" I've never heard the song since those days. Any way the gramophone went, I think we made too much noise.

* *This was Violet Carson who later went on to play Ena Sharples in Coronation St.*

"Another thing I can remember was the old chipped enamel mugs we had our tea in, which sometimes was very weak or black as ink. We could listen on the radio to the detective Dick Barton, that's if we behaved ourselves. In bad weather, in winter we would have rubber sheets put on the beds of those at the front of the ward, which was open to all weathers. There were no shutters or anything to protect you or to keep the rain off. One bad winter we had a lot of snow on our beds so we made snowballs to throw at each other. If we could, we would throw the snowball at the roof over a boy's bed, so when it thawed it would drip on them.

"After tea, at night some of us would help to roll bandages with a wooden roller for the nurses and some evenings the night nurse would give some of us a slice of cold toast; that was something really nice. We had a teacher that came to teach us how to make things, like raffia baskets, string shopping bags, sea grass stools, and make scrap-books out of black and red paper from the x-rays.

"For the boys who couldn't get out of bed we had a modesty blanket, which we always kept over us in bed, because you couldn't wear pyjamas over the iron frame you were fastened on.

"I was in Kirbymoorside Hospital, for over three years, 1945-48, having treatment on my hip. I was stretched out on an iron frame for quite some time, put in plaster-of-paris from under my arms down my leg to my ankle. When that was taken off, I had a leather casing put around my body and leg. All this treatment was to make sure that I didn't bend my leg at the hip. My friend Michael Mawe, who also came from Hull, was in the next bed to me for most of the time we were in hospital. He had the disease in his knee which was bent. He had weights put on his leg to try and straighten it, but it couldn't be put straight, so Michael had to have his leg taken off from above the knee.

"I was transferred to Beverley Road Hospital in Hull, in Spring 1948, as I was having trouble with kidney stones, which I had to have taken out. I was told it was the result of lying flat in bed for so long. I had various treatments in the Hull Hospital, kidney treatment and bone grafts over the next three years."

It wasn't only youngsters who found themselves in need of the expertise of The Adela Shaw Hospital. Local man **Peter Stockdale** had just finished his apprenticeship as a mechanic for Russell's Engineering when he developed TB in his spine. Initially he was cared for at home and received streptomycin injections from Dr Stuart, the local doctor. Peter recalls that the needles were blunt and he often offered to sharpen them, an offer that was not taken up. Then he was transferred to Scarborough where the injections were less painful. A plaster cast was made of his back and front and this was put onto

Left: Peter Stockdale at The Adela Shaw with his brother John.

Right: Jimmy Marshall, appearing in one of the hospital pantos

a frame supported by trestles; however when he needed the injections he was tipped out of one cast into another which was less than ideal. His auntie, Win Rickaby, knew Dr Adamson through the Red Cross and she got Dr Crockatt to see Peter and to take on his case. Back at Kirbymoorside the cast was immediately removed by Jackie Baxter and replaced with something more secure. Godfrey Woof came down and measured Peter for a steel frame, which resembled a scarecrow. Within the frame Peter was strapped down using splints and padding, so that his ribcage was the highest point of his body. Moving about was impossible and he spent 11 months like this to prevent the TB damaging his spine. To try to make life a little more bearable the bed was raised by blocks so he could see around him and they moved the locker so he could reach it with his arms. During an eclipse he was even wheeled over to the window so he could get a view of it. Sister Place was in charge of his ward, Ward II, where she ruled with a firm hand and had the respect of everyone around. Others he can remember being there were the night staff Miss Wardle, Miss Denney and Mrs Garbutt - the night orderlies and Molly Moody, the daytime ward maid, who was always willing to pop up street and bring back requests for the older ones – permitted or otherwise. To pass time Peter did embroidery and other crafts, whilst Michael Potter and John Griffin, who both suffered from haemophilia, were caught by Sister Place carefully making model aeroplanes using razor sharp knives - she was not happy. With Jimmy Marshall's encouragement the boys continued to make the planes, albeit carefully, and a group of model plane enthusiasts visited in 1952 and 1953 to give the boys demonstrations. Having survived Sister Place's wrath and the knives, Michael Potter later went on to work with Mr Archie Crawford [Clocky Crawford] a local jeweller and watchmaker. Another local boy in the hospital was Edward Atkinson from Lastingham, where he received treatment for dislocated hips. Several of the children used to write and paint using their toes. Tom Pashby, 16 years, was another older patient who had damaged himself by falling in the family's fishing boat. He was immobilised in aeroplane splints and had to be laid down slowly to adjust to life on a frame. However he still managed to pinch the last sandwich on a plate by putting his foot on it. After his treatment Tom got back to Scarborough and continued fishing in the family business.

The orderly Jimmy Marshall was very good to the boys, and Peter especially being of similar age and background. Ever the joker Jimmy was known for injecting fruit and chocolate with cascara [a laxative] and the staff were always very wary of stealing any of his chocolates. The boys thought this was great. Over Christmas 1956-57, all the children who could not go home either through illness or having nowhere else to go, were brought into one ward and had a Christmas party with plenty of good food and presents. Visitors were allowed and Peter got many young local men who said they had come to see how he was doing but were equally occupied with the young nurses. One incident related to this was a request from Sister Dixon, the night sister, who was constantly battling to keep the girls and boys apart after hours. She brought her torch to Peter to fix having thrown it into a hedge to chase a local suitor away.

Fred King - Teacher

Mr King was responsible for schooling in Ward II and Peter remembers one boy from Leeds, Brian Wine. Previously a very active young man, he was struck down by polio and was paralysed except for the use of one arm. Despite this he could hold a boiled egg and eat it by himself using a spoon. His teacher recognised his academic abilities too and gave him extra tuition allowing Brian to pass a series of exams whilst at The Adela Shaw.

After 11 months on his back immobilised Peter had to learn to walk again. Godfrey made him a customised steel-framed leather jacket to support him, padded to try and prevent sores. All the time he had been laid flat he had not got a single bedsore – a testament to the care of the nurses. The only time it happened was whilst moving about wearing this jacket. The nurses prevented sores by rubbing soap into their hands and massaging it into the patient's skin. This was then patted dry and methylated spirits dabbed on top which would evaporate and dry. These types of patients were particularly susceptible and bedsores were to be avoided at all costs as they took months to heal. Another unexpected complaint which arose from being still for so long was that once Peter began to move about he suffered with pains in his feet, to such an extent that he could not sleep. Dr Adamson told him that this was caused by the tiny bones and muscles in the feet trying to align themselves again. The cure was simple – the nurses walked him to the sluice room where he soaked his feet in warm and cold water alternately. He was wheeled back to bed and enjoyed a good night's sleep. He was off work for two years but eventually returned to work for the same firm.

Cerebral Palsy Unit in the former Isolation Block

Maureen Fawcett

Those recovering from the immobilisation needed aftercare and they worked with the nurses and the physiotherapists who were based at the hospital. The physios came from near and far – including a Finnish physiotherapist Miss R Westerberg in 1950 and Anita Sundholm and Karita Lonqvist from Sweden in 1951. In 1950 **Maureen Fawcett [Precious]** and **Dorothy Cook [Walker]** began work at The Adela Shaw Hospital. Maureen started working on the wards as an orderly and Dorothy was working with the aftercare sister Miss Braemer who had been there for 20 years. When it was decided to set up a dedicated unit for patients with mobility issues the hospital established the Cerebral Palsy Unit [CPU] in the old Isolation Ward at the top of the site. Here they worked not only with those who had to get walking but also with the children who would not recover such as those with spina bifida, muscular dystrophy, rheumatoid arthritis and congenital hydrocephalus. A few children with hydrocephalus still suffered with the enlarged heads caused by the excessive fluid, something which thankfully today is treated before such complications occur. Dorothy and Maureen worked in the gymnasium as well as the CPU, where the children could experience some freedom from the confines of their chairs and wards. The children were still in the large wooden wheelchairs, made to measure by Mr Porritt, and the hospital had specially adapted tables made to allow the children to be placed inside so they had some freedom to move but were still secure. Others would play and stretch on mattresses

Dorothy Cook

whilst some would have specific treatment. They would give electric treatment to stimulate muscles, short-wave and ultraviolet treatments for skin conditions and shingles. They would also use massage to relax muscles and assist the children to relearn to walk by using the parallel bars, which was possible even after years on the fixed frames. The children would benefit from the constant care at the hospital and when they would go home of the holidays, often they had regressed slightly. Swimming was another form of therapy used and they would take the children to Welburn Hall, all very physically demanding work. No lifts or special equipment was used in the early days, they just had to work together and lift them as best they could. Elizabeth Coverdale [Kay] worked for the hospital physiotherapy unit from

Afternoon rest in the gym

1960 - 1970. Others remembered there were Margaret Thorsen, Mrs Egerton, Ms Bainbridge, Mrs Popperwell and Mrs Fisher to name only a few. Neither Maureen nor Dorothy lived on site and they worked during the day. Despite this they were subject to the same rules as the nursing staff. They would take their meals in the nurses' dining room and Maureen recalls being reprimanded by Matron Lillie for walking with her arms folded. The children there were taught in the CPU and the teacher was a Mrs Preston. They would do the same activities as those on the wards and do embroidery, craft work if they were able. In the afternoon they would take a

Maureen Fawcett took some of the children from The Adela Shaw to watch the guests arrive at the wedding reception of Catherine Worsley and The Duke Of Kent in 1961 at Hovingham Hall.

rest in the gym but very little sleeping took place – children will be children.

During the holidays they would help on the wards with the resident patients, cleaning and bathing them. They also took them out on trips away to places including the Benelux Festival in Scarborough. Here the children encountered Jimmy Savile in a gold lamé suit. He was visiting his mother and got on the bus to talk to the children. Matron Lillie was not impressed. They would take them out on picnics and lay them out on the back seat of the bus to get them about. The affection felt by the staff of the hospital for the children is apparent; even after all these years both Dorothy and Maureen can remember many of the names and faces of the children they cared for.

From the age of 16 years the nurses were expected to take on roles and responsibilities which today would not be allowed. Training for these nurses meant starting with the very basics – cleaning and scrubbing the wards, damp dusting and disinfecting bathrooms and surfaces, fetching and carrying whatever and whenever necessary. All the girls lived on site and were under the direct authority of the Matron and below her the sisters. They had to help patients to the toilets, wash and dress them on a morning with the assistance of the orderlies. The rules they had to follow were strict and there was a real hierarchy in place. A junior nurse was expected to give priority to a senior and if something needed doing the junior would have to do it before her superior. They all took turns at the jobs throughout the hospital including the theatre where they would observe operations.

Maud Cram (†) with the evacuated patients at Welburn Hall

With the outbreak of WWII women were expected to join the war effort. **Maud Cram** had been working as a nanny for a solicitor in York and then chose to join the nursing auxiliary in the hospitals. She did 13 weeks basic training at York County Hospital before spending two years at the Children's Hospital in Knaresborough. After she married Harold Cram in 1942 she transferred to Kirbymoorside and The Adela Shaw Hospital to be with his family whilst he was abroad with the Royal Engineers. She went to work at the hospital and was posted to the Welburn Hall Annexe. She began on a salary of 15 shillings a week and had to live in with board and lodgings included. She spent a year based with children who had been evacuated from some of the Kirkbymoorside wards, which were needed for military cases. She remembers Matron Poole as very strict but fair and she enjoyed being at a distance from Matron's watchful eye. The children were treated in two wards - one for the boys and one for the girls, with around 40 in total. The wards were in two large downstairs rooms and the main wooden staircase was blocked off. The nurses slept upstairs and had to use the back staircase with Sister Duffy in charge of them all. She remembers being on night duty with Sister Nancy Pickard and both of them awaiting the arrival of the "Grey Lady." The Grey Lady is the ghost known to haunt Welburn Hall –

she would come out of a bedroom, down the main staircase through the French doors at the front, across the lawn down to the lake where her dogs had been buried. Fortunately nothing was seen that night. However another night the excitement came from a more sinister source – the same one that had brought Dr Crockatt rushing to Welburn. The Hall was bombarded with German incendiary bombs and the children had to be hidden under their beds. The surrounding corn fields were set alight but the Hall and the children were thankfully undamaged.

The Nursing Auxiliaries wore a uniform which included a blue stripy dress with a long white apron. They wore white linen squares which were tied tight around the head and fastened in such a way as to form a bow at the back. They were only occasionally visited by the doctors and Matron Poole so they had relative freedom. From Welburn she was transferred to the Nawton Towers Annexe; again giving the staff distance from the hospital's tight regime. She was there 11 weeks over the summer of 1944. Sister Deighton was in charge and the gardens offered them an abundant crop of soft fruit and vegetables – all available to the staff and children, which resulted in many wonderful meals being prepared. In June 1944 she received a call to pack her bags and go onto night duty back in Kirbymoorside. That night the hospital filled with hundreds of injured soldiers brought in from the D-Day Landings in need of treatment – even the gymnasium was requisitioned to cater for the overwhelming numbers of casualties. The soldiers did not stay long and soon some children returned. Maud loved working on the babies ward and particularly

Maud Cram (left) outside the Babies Ward with Sister Hardy (seated right)

remembers baby Janni – whose parents were Swedish, making her a real bonny baby. The only drawback for her was that she would get attached to the babies and of course they all had to go home. Very few stayed more than a few months. Wartime rations were issued on a Monday by Mrs Charlton the cook. The butter and sugar were kept in the dining room and had to last the week. Back at the main hospital Maud was treated the same as all the other nurses and lived in the Nurses Home. Despite the fact she was a married woman aged 24 years, she still had to ask permission and seek late passes if she wanted to leave the hospital grounds.

Her duties on the wards were general nursing care for the children – feeding washing and taking temperatures. The only thing the auxiliary nurses did not do were the children's dressings. Night duties in winter she remembers were bitterly cold. They were allowed to wear a cardigan and would spend some time sitting round the heater in the office. The children were kept wrapped up in red blankets whilst the open shuttered windows did not have any glass in them.

As well as the children, Maud recalls several local accident victims who were brought to the hospital for treatment in 1944 - 1945. One accident involved a tank at "Mousy Hole", the locals name for the dip in the road outside Welburn Hall. One of the soldiers was brought in suffering from severe burns. Another time an airman testing a glider down at Slingsby's was brought in after it crashed and Mr Kit Fletcher arrived having sawn a finger off in his wood yard, situated in West End. She finally left the hospital in 1945 at the same time as her husband was demobbed. For her Dr Crockatt was a god and Dr Adamson was simply wonderful – this impression of the two key figures at the Adela Shaw and the work they did in the hospital has remained with her for over 65 years and is a tribute to their dedication.

Winifred [Win] Mitchell [White] came to work at the Adela Shaw from Middlesbrough in August 1944, and was immediately whisked off in Matron Poole's Austin 7 car with two others to start work at the Nawton Towers Annexe. She was struck by the isolation of the place and the beauty of the heather in bloom. After being issued with their uniforms and being off-duty; unsure what to do next, they decided to go for a walk and changed before they went out. Called into Sister Grey's office later, they were reprimanded for wandering about looking for boys! Sister Grey was a large ginger-haired lady who wore a big sister's hat which she had a tendency to flick. When the snows came the Annexe was cut-off and the water tanks in the courtyard froze. This was their only water supply so they had to defrost the tap with kettles. These water tanks were part of the defence measures put in place in case of enemy invasion.

She recalls that there were around 40 boys and girls in four bedrooms that had been converted into wards and that on occasions Lady Feversham would sweep into the wards from their private quarters to collect clothes from the huge walk-in wardrobes. The children had their own teacher at Nawton, Ms Brenda Downes who was from Bradford and the visitors were bussed up once a month and stayed for the day to see their children. If they were lucky the nurses got a ride back into town or else they had to walk or cycle the six miles to Kirbymoorside. After three months Win came back to the main hospital and remembers the convalescing soldiers on the wards. Not every nurse was allowed on these wards as the soldiers would be very different patients to handle.

Nurse Mitchell, Nurse Fox, Nurse Aconley, with Nurse Pygas in front

Olga Fox [Hammond] started at The Adela Shaw in September 1945 also at the age of 16½ on a salary of £2 10/- a month including accommodation on site. With a day off per week and a weekend every month, she began at the Kirkbymoorside hospital whilst soldiers were there – tales of maggots cleaning the wounds of those men who were brought from the Dunkirk evacuations still fresh in the staff's memory and the Polish and Canadian soldiers were still in town. Staffing shortages meant that the Matron, Miss Bedwell had to ask her sisters to work, both of whom were over 70 years old. After very little introduction Nurse Fox was cleaning the floors using sand mixed with Izal disinfectant, cleaning the sluices and working her way up the tasks. All the wards were Nightingale type wards with the patients' beds in rows clearly visible to the staff from either end. The veranda doors were kept open night and day and the children had to have rubber covers on them to keep the damp away. During winter the boys would snowball each other and the nurses would wear long blue gowns and gloves whilst on night duty; in summer the children would be awake early as the daylight hit them. She remembers the bandages had to be washed and the boys would help roll them up before they went to be sterilised.

A lot of the children who came in were from very poor backgrounds and often they had been hidden away within the family home. Knowledge and the ability to cope with these disabilities were very different to today, and when the children arrived at the hospital they were in need of cleaning, bathing and feeding. They also had to be clothed and when they returned home it was not unknown for these clothes to stay behind and the staff had to provide more. Often the first few days were very traumatic for the children, but as they got used to the care and attention they would open up and settle onto the wards. For a few children they would never leave and would remain within the care system throughout their lives, whilst others would progress and move onto full active lives. For others having spent five years in the hospital without seeing their families the idea of returning home was not always welcome.

The staff would have 15 minutes for their lunch but Mrs Charlton would often supplement their rations with hot mugs of cocoa, sugar sandwiches and bread and dripping. The work was very physical and the nurses were often tired. Matron Bedwell was also very strict and would inspect the wards, everyone had to stand by the beds and she would check everything was in order. She had a checklist of things to be done which she did everyday without fail.

After doing her two years Olga went on to do her General Nursing Certificate at Scarborough General Hospital and returned to The Adela Shaw as a sister. One incident which she still recalls and made the papers involved an Irish doctor based at the hospital. There had been an Irish horse racing event in the field adjacent to the hospital - known as a "flapping race" and the subsequent celebrations led to rather boisterous behaviour, which in turn attracted the attention of the police.

Sister Judy Eason [Pickard] came to The Adela Shaw Hospital in 1949 as a sister just as the polio epidemic hit Kirkbymoorside; she had taken her training at the Middlesbrough General Hospital and initially took charge of the girls' ward before transferring to the Babies Ward after Sister Jean Bowes left. Sister Fox was her staff nurse and she had care of babies from the age of a few months old upwards. Matron Bedwell was in charge when she first arrived and took exception to Sister Eason's method of aligning the wheels of the cots inwards as she had been taught at Middlesbrough. Matron would use her stick to knock

Nurse Conning and the boys on a picnic

them out of line, because she could. Judy also had a never-ending battle with keeping a ward full of children quiet and often would read bedtime stories to try to lull them to sleep. At Christmas she along with the nurses and children would spend hours making decorations and flowers to go up in the wards. During the summer months the babies and children would go outside, frames and all, and they had to be careful the children did not get sunburn. She recalls that the atmosphere in the hospital was warm and friendly, even Dr Adamson's dog Ling was welcome on the wards.

Nurse Margaret Conning [Bartram] started in 1953 and vividly remembers her first stint in the theatre. The operations done at The Adela Shaw were bloodless; that is where a tourniquet was put around the limb and tightened to stop the flow of blood. This meant the limb looked yellow and strange. The anaesthetic was applied by Dr Adamson. There was a modern style machine to do this however she never trusted it enough to use it and preferred the use of a mask and ether - "rag and bottle" as it was known. There was a real art to keeping the patient under anaesthetic whilst remaining awake yourself. This type of field surgery had it origins in the battle zones, but was used to excellent effect at The Adela Shaw. The instruments that Dr Crockatt used resembled those in the workshops with mallets and chisels. Everything had to be sterilised by packing large bins with the glass syringes, needles, swabs as well as hammers and chisels. These bins went into a steam autoclave and all these had to be laid out by Sister before the operation. The gloves would be tested by filling them with water and then, once dry, they had to be dusted with talcum powder to allow them to be worn. Dr Crockatt once ordered a new saw and was very proud of it –

Stephen Thompson the only problem was it was too big for the autoclave. The only way to sterilise it was to put it into the oven in the kitchens, making sure that a large note went onto the doors to warn cook! On a very few occasions Dr Crockatt would not wear gloves, but instead applied a special barrier cream to allow him to feel the joints accurately during the operation. The staff were not allowed to wear any jewellery and they had to scrub up to their elbows.

All the nurses remember the noise of the operations, with much hammering and sawing. Others remember that some of the surgeons had favourite music – Mr Quinlin would always have *Housewife's Choice* on the radio and was partial to packets of Polos. The dresses worn by the nurses were described as thin and green and one Polish doctor, the anaesthetist Dr Lagowski, had the knack of undoing the bras of the unsuspecting nurse, much to their embarrassment. No offence was ever meant or taken. The operating room was run by the theatre sister - for many years this was Sister Bowes - however it was the job of the theatre orderly to collect and return the child patients on a flat trolley with no sides. Jimmy Marshall was one of those who took on this role and he was always very good with the children. When he retired Stephen Thompson took over and is remembered by many as being a very good and kindly man. Ann Jones [Wilson] recalls going to the hospital in 1963 and Mr Thompson cut off her plaster from her arm using the infamous oscillating saw and the ease with which he reassured her it would not hurt - a memory shared by many others.

Nurse Milestone (left) Nurse Jane Edwards

Nurse June Milestone [Cook] went to The Adela Shaw in 1955 before going on to take her nursing certificate at Scarborough and then midwifery at Middlesbrough. She was on Ward II and can still remember many of the boys and girls there. She would often catch the children trying to wriggle themselves into such a position that they could pick things off the floors, even though their legs would be strapped up with pulleys. The children were never given any painkillers or antibiotics, even though they had been developed during

70

the war. Despite this there were no real complications with infections. The only problems that she can recall would be after certain children came back from holidays at home and the callipers had rubbed sores and they had to be deloused and fed back to health. This was not necessarily caused by

Many of the old faces from a hospital show in the early fifties

neglect but the conditions would be so different at home the care they needed was just not available. During the summer holidays those patients resident at Welburn Hall would come to the hospital and they were difficult to entertain as these children were used to far more freedom than the wards could offer. The speed that could be reached by children in callipers was as fast as those without and the children quickly adapted to the extra weight. She remembers they liked to listen to *"Six Five Special"*, one of the first pop programmes on the TV. During the long nights she remembers putting the ribbons from the girls on top of the urn to dry and would pull them back and forth to iron them ready for the morning.

No name tags were worn and it was unheard of for anyone to be addressed by their first names on the wards even if they started at the same time. The idea of having any kind of personal conversations whilst on the wards was unheard of – it simply did not happen. The staff had their own sewing machine in the nurses' home and everyone would help each other to make outfits for the dances. They also had their own laundry bags and everything in it would go off and come back starched even the underwear! The staff also had their own butter dish and it was common for those on nights to pinch the butter from their colleagues who were on day shifts. They would prepare snacks for the children on a night-time and Nurse Conning fell foul of the boys' mischief when one of them asked for scrambled eggs. The next morning Sister Fox advised Nurse Conning that the eggs she had done were not to be used as they were on special diets.

Hospital Staff in 1960/61

Jennifer Bailey [Robinson] and her contemporaries **Pat Gullen [Wigley] Eleanor Wheatley** and **Joyce Spink [Hammond]** all remember life at the hospital as both hard work and good fun. Hierarchy in the hospital was strong and often they would have to walk the length of the ward to answer the phone and then walk all the way back to fetch the person needed. Running was not allowed. The junior nurse would have to put coal onto the fires and was expected to give way in the corridors. When they were going out to a local dance they would need to get a pass from Matron and often travelled in the old ambulance affectionately known as 'Josephine' driven by Stephen Welford. On other occasions they would use Henry Bentley's converted hearse and Mike Pulleyn's taxi, who also had a dance band called the Four Aces, and later Hodgson's taxi. They were allowed one late pass until 10 pm a month and if going to a dance then it was extended until 12 midnight; anything else would require a letter from the parents.

Joyce lived at Nawton and went home to sleep on nights until Sister became aware and she got into trouble for it. If they were too late back then they had their own ways of getting back into the Nurses' home. Along the side of the site were fields and the buildings were all on one level. Open windows meant the cows could be heard coughing during the night but with the help of a laundry basket it also meant an easy entrance for both nurses and late night visitors. The local boys were often around. They would call on a night-time and try to chat through the windows and offer to fetch chips for those on night duty. Sister Dixon used to check the linen cupboards and sluices to find the hidden male callers and was even known to rattle the bushes with an umbrella to flush out those hidden. Matron Lillie was not unaware and the sisters were ever vigilant; the smell of chips was often a giveaway. No boys were allowed past the hospital gates – or the "pearly gates" as they were also known. Many of the nurses found their future husbands in the town and stayed on to raise families here; however they would have to ask Matron's permission to marry if under 21.

One such nurse who met her husband in Kirby was **Matilda "Tilly" Anderson**. She came to Kirkbymoorside in 1926 from Hetton-le-Hole nr Sunderland and was one of the first to work in the newly opened Yorkshire Children's Hospital. She met her husband-to-be Frank Simpson at the gates of the hospital – he was working at Hodgson's Garage opposite the entrance. Frank was to encounter Matron Poole in an official capacity when an accident involving a motorbike engine severed all the fingers of his right hand at the first knuckle. They rushed him to the hospital where Matron Poole greeted them with the words "so where are the fingers?" An ambulance was dispatched to retrieve them but they could not be re-attached. Instead the skin was used to cover the ends and they eventually formed into fingers. However because Frank would favour his left hand the muscles became distorted and overdeveloped. When Godfrey Woof saw him he immediately set to and designed a special splint to correct the muscles. Years later history repeated itself when their son Eric James Simpson met a student nurse called **Caroline Slade [Simpson]** at the local dance and they too later married and Eric continued his military service for some time until his discharge on 11 June 1973. Caroline and their two children served with him for most of his time in the military.

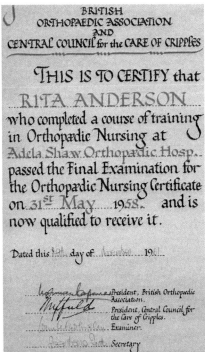

Rita Anderson [Gibson] started at The Adela Shaw in 1956 and she came from Scarborough to do her two years orthopaedic nursing certificate before going back to Scarborough to do the three years training which enabled her to return in 1962 as a sister. Sister Tutor Clark taught the nurses all the basics of human physiology and anatomy, as well as nursing techniques. The lectures were delivered in the Recreation Room and the nurses would spend a month en bloc training. The more specialist lectures would be delivered by Dr Crockatt, Dr Adamson and the other visiting surgeons. For those doing the orthopaedic nursing it was essential they do plaster-room work and theatre work was seen as desirable. Before receiving their orthopaedic certification the nurses were expected to take general training or become State Enrolled Assistant Nurses.

In later years the hospital's focus shifted from a specialist unit to a general hospital as Polio and TB were largely eradicated with the vaccination programme. With it the specialist knowledge and nursing at The Adela Shaw was lost. By the mid 1960s the hospital was catering for the adult patients and would treat anything from tonsils, adenoids and bunions to hip

replacements. The old-fashioned regimes fell away and it gradually adopted the style and methods of the central hospital at Scarborough. In 1958 Dr Crockatt retired from the hospital after 32 years service as the first and only resident superintendent. He and his wife moved to Arran in Scotland and he died in 1964 aged 66 years.

After Dr Crockatt left, the hospital relied on visiting consultants from Scarborough Hospital. However the age of the buildings was beginning to have a serious effect on the safety of the wards. A decision was taken to close The Adela Shaw Hospital and transfer the long stay patients to a new orthopaedic centre which was to be built at Cross Lane Scarborough.

Dr Crockatt and his sister-in-law following his retirement

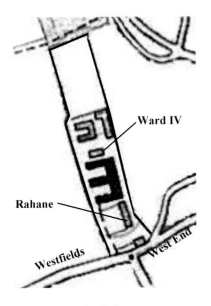

Hospital site in 1960s

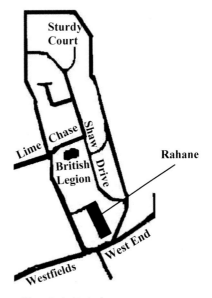

Hospital site today

The remaining patients went to the hospitals closest to their homes. This decision brought a fierce 18 month battle with the Health Authorities and questions were asked in the House of Commons. Eventually the concession made was the retention of an outpatient's facility. This was based at "Rahane" the former residence of Dr Crockatt. It offered physiotherapy, X-rays and visiting specialists. So in 1970 the gates closed on The Adela Shaw site for good. The land was sold off and despite interest by local groups, the site became a housing development with the exception of Ward IV. This was leased by the British Legion Club and they are still based there today. The outpatients department closed in the 1990s and the iron gates were taken away. The only visible markers left behind are two of the impassive stone gate posts, whilst "Rahane" and the stone cottages are now private houses.

This story began with a generous offer a lady - Mrs Adela Shaw and ended with Dr Howard Ludbrook Crockatt, who brought the project to life and carried it further than anyone else could.

A visionary and a man before his time

A man held in high esteem by his colleagues and patients alike

A man who understood the needs and concerns of the children and who was driven by his desire to cure and ease their suffering

That is the history of Kirkbymoorside's Children's Hospital.

**Sisters Farr, Eason, Miss Braemer, Sisters Carr, Hanby
June 1949**

The **Kirkbymoorside History Group** began
life in 1998 with a few people who wanted to preserve the
rapidly disappearing knowledge from our small market town. As
a result the **Kirkbymoorside** history project was formed and the
group published a series of booklets on all aspects of the
town's history - The Kirkbymoorside Times.

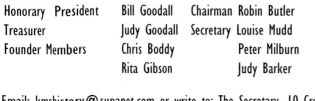

Honorary President	Bill Goodall	Chairman Robin Butler
Treasurer	Judy Goodall	Secretary Louise Mudd
Founder Members	Chris Boddy	Peter Milburn
	Rita Gibson	Judy Barker

Email: kmshistory@supanet.com or write to: The Secretary, 10 Crown Square, Kirkbymoorside,
York YO62 6AY

We would like to thank all those who gave their time and effort in speaking to us and to
thank Ann Wilson for her invaluable support in researching and compiling the booklet. We also
would like to thank the Ryedale Folk Museum, Malton Hospital and the County Records Office
for allowing us access to their source material - namely

- The Adela Shaw Hospital General & Directors' Minute Books 1924 - 1947
- Annual Board of Governors' Reports 1926 -1946
- Matron's Log Book 1949 - 1970
- Newspaper Cuttings Book courtesy of Malton Hospital
- Hayes Photographic Collection - Ryedale Folk Museum Hutton le Hole

Coming Soon: A pictorial archive of the wards of The Adela Shaw Hospital
"The Life of a Church" - The History Of All Saints Church, Kirkbymoorside
"Kirkbymoorside Times 2010 - Revised and Updated".

Group shot on Page 71 - Class of 1960/61

Back Row L to R: Helen Johnson, Jennifer Bailey, Mary Johnson, Lynn Gibson, Marie
Shipley, Sylvia Harland, ?, Duna Brizelle, Eleanor Wheatley, Sue Lythe

Middle Row L to R: Maureen Milner, Sister Robertson, Sister Frances Place, Mr
Quinlin (surgeon), Dr K Adamson, Mr Tupman (surgeon), Sister Jean Bowes, Ted
Clark

Front Row L to R: ? Joyce Spink, ? Roslyn Porritt, Mavis Shepherd, Pat Gullen, Chris
Hodgson